Britain Should Join the Euro:

Essays on the 10th Anniversary of the Launch of the European Single Currency

Table of Contents

Preface

These papers are the result of a discussion convened by Peter Sutherland on the 4th of November 2008. Their publication is intended to help place the case for Britain joining the Euro back upon the political agenda and to provide the beginnings of an ongoing forum for its promotion. Additional papers addressing further aspects of the matter and more detailed analyses will follow over the coming months in the hope of creating a rallying point for more weighty interests to find the courage of their convictions.

John Stevens

Summary
Britain Should Join the Euro:
Essays on the 10th Anniversary of the
Launch of the European Single Currency

Published by: John Stevens
Edited by: Graham Bishop, Willem Buiter,
               Brendan Donnelly and Will Hutton

This report is intended to relaunch the campaign for Britain joining the Euro. It does so in the following terms:

- The British political class as a whole has failed to anticipate the economic crisis, the worst for several generations, just as it has failed to resolve, for over a generation, the principal strategic issue facing the country – the nature of our relationship with the European Union.
- In particular, it has failed now to understand that joining the Euro is a vital element in the strategy which is necessary for Britain to get through the crisis and rebuild our prosperity on sound foundations.
- This is principally because Britain needs the credibility of membership of the Eurozone in order to secure sufficient foreign investment to fund our current account and fiscal deficits. The government especially needs to prove that it is committed, in the long term, to living within its means by giving up the power to print the currency in which it borrows.
- Without the prospect of Euro membership we will not be able to finance the fiscal stimulus necessary to mitigate the crisis and could face a full-blown loss of international credit worthiness, which would be a catastrophe far larger, even, than that which we suffered at the time of the IMF bailout in 1976.
- To rebuild our economy in the medium term, we must reinforce our areas of competitive advantage in international services, especially financial services and, more generally, secure the continuation, as far as possible, of international free trade.
- One of the key lessons of the crisis is that an international financial centre such as the City of London will only be able to flourish if it is supported by a lender of last resort in a global reserve currency. The City's future now depends on our joining the Euro.
- Given the level of government support for various sectors of their national economies which this crisis has brought on, international free trade and the revival of Western growth now depend on a return to a stable currency regime, such

as prevailed before the break up of Bretton Woods. This requires an accord between the Dollar and the Euro, which would be greatly facilitated by Britain joining the Single Currency.

- The crisis has made necessary a dramatic improvement in the international regulation of financial services. Britain's influence now over this process would be greatly enhanced by making clear our intention to join the Euro.

- European governments and, indeed, the new US administration, would welcome Britain joining the Euro within the next three years. The barrier to membership lies with British public opinion whose hostility is the legacy of the abject failure of leadership on European questions of our political class.

- A representative democracy can only function properly and be legitimate if its political class exercises leadership. Until our democratic representatives rediscover their duty to lead, rather than follow, to anticipate events, rather than react to them, it falls to ordinary concerned citizens to make the case for Britain joining the Euro.

British Membership of the Euro:
Time to Think Again?

I believe it is time to put the case for joining the Euro back on the agenda for policy discussion. When the case was last investigated and, with the publication of the Treasury's Report on the Five Tests, effectively terminated, the case for not joining was strong. Now I believe that the case is much weaker, perhaps decisively so. A number of important factors have changed. As this is the time for quoting Keynes, it is worth bearing in mind the reproof he directed at someone who criticised the seeming inconstancy of his expressed views: "When the facts change I change my mind. What do you do?"

13
Michael Artis

First and most important, when the case for Euro was last rehearsed, British citizens could be excused for following the wise old American saying "If it ain't broke, don't fix it". This well-founded attitude was based on a long period of increasing prosperity and moderate inflation. It was reflected in a long run of predominantly negative answers to the question, as administered by polling organizations, "if there were a referendum on joining the Euro would you answer Yes or No to the question 'Should Britain join the Euro?' The American adage hardly applies today. Attitudes towards joining the Euro seem likely to change as a result.

One of the ingredients in the long run of prosperity was undoubtedly the high value of the exchange rate of the pound against the Euro (and other currencies). Once again, things have changed. Where the exchange rate was arguably too high before, now it is arguably too low. It was difficult to recommend locking into the Euro at the rates prevailing in the late '90s through to 2007 and it would be wise to await some appreciation before locking in now – but that some fall in the exchange rate can be welcomed is hardly beyond dispute. Still, while we are on the subject of the exchange rate, it is not just quibbles about whether the rate is right or not at a particular time that should count. Rather, the lesson that might be learnt is that the recent behaviour of the exchange rate gives little ground for optimism about its role as a stabilizer when Britain's exchange rate is floating. In fact there have been a number of studies which seem to show that the exchange rate may, for many countries, be just as much a source of shocks as a stabilizer of them. Usually the countries identified as those for whom the negative verdict on the stabilizing properties of the exchange rate is appropriate are small countries for whom the gyrations of the foreign exchange market overwhelm the potential for stabilization of domestic monetary policy. Now Britain is not as small as some of those countries, but recent events do not encourage one to position the economy so that it is a victim of the market's unreasoning tendency to move by leaps and bounds on news of the slightest change in circumstance.

Michael Artis

Another important lesson that we have been able to learn is that European Central Bank policy – contrary to some early hypercritical analyses (mostly emanating from the City of London) – has been well-considered and well-conducted. A recent very thorough investigation of the matter (issued as working paper of the National Bureau of Economic Research) has concluded that "it is hard to find major fault with what they [the ECB] have done over the past decade". It is fair to say that had the UK joined the Euro a decade ago the great success of the institution – even given participation by gifted UK central bankers – could be in doubt, such would have been the contrary pulls of British and continental interests.

Here is another area in which things have changed –if not decisively – then quite lot. In the past the business cycle experience of the UK was not closely aligned with that of the Eurozone countries. When the UK largely escaped the backwash of the 2000-2001 dotcom bubble burst and consequent recession in the United States, the countries of the Eurozone experienced a prolonged period of slow growth. For long the "UK business cycle idiosyncrasy" marked it out as unsuitable in a monetary policy partnership with the continental economies – a single monetary policy could not have been suitable for both while business cycles are not closely synchronized. Moreover it was remarked that no single UK region showed an affiliation with the Eurozone countries (unlike the case for even the more marginal of the Eurozone countries, where it was possible to find one or more regions in tune with the European cycle. What seems to have been happening is that the force of globalization has driven all business cycles closer together – there may be a separate Europeanization effect, but if so this is obscured by globalization. On these grounds then the prospect of a single monetary policy is no longer so disturbing.

Some have argued that Iceland's fate is an instructive pathology for the UK to observe. Size – or relative lack of it – is certainly one of the features of today's landscape that stands out. Whilst the size of the country – even when measured in GDP relative to that of the rest of the world has not changed much, it has certainly fallen in recent years. More certainly still, the financial globalization of the world and the size of mobile capital funds make smaller countries more vulnerable than they were. It's not likely that this clock will be turned back much, if at all. This means that one of the attractions of joining the Euro is simply that of the security of its large size.

In conclusion, we are half a decade on from the publication of the Treasury's negative report on the five tests. A lot has changed in that time. I have spelt out a number of ways in which things have changed – not a lot in each and every case but cumulatively. It is time to put the Euro back on the policy agenda.

Michael Artis - Welsh Assembly Government Visiting Research Professor at the University of Swansea. Fellow of the British Academy and Research Fellow of the Centre for Economic Policy Research.

Winning Hearts and Minds:
The Battle for British Public Opinion

"I know that British Euro membership faces large political hurdles…
newspaper editors would have to be bribed"

Wolfgang Munchau (FT 17/11/2008)

"I cannot refrain from the hope that in future England's statesmen
will take up the cause of   European peace and civilisation in friendly
cooperation with other states"

A.F. Pribram "England and the international policy of the European
powers"

17
Richard Bassett

In the sombre crisis-ridden last days of peace in 1914, the British Foreign Secretary, Sir Edward Grey, was repeatedly pressed by his French and Russian colleagues to state categorically that Britain would be faithful to its Entente with France and warn Germany that she would have to reckon with war with England. Each time Grey skilfully maintained his room for manoeuvre and resisted the pressure. Even as late as August 1st he could argue forcefully that London could not abandon neutrality "for the simple reason that public opinion would not sanction any other course". At the Cabinet meeting that Sunday, a clear majority were against any involvement in the looming conflict. Both the City, many of whose prominent bankers were of German stock, and much of the media were against engagement. Grey kept his freedom of action until the end. But the end was not to be very far away. Four days later London had declared war on Germany.

However dramatic the present financial crisis, it is on a smaller scale, mercifully, than 1914 but the question arises as to whether British pragmatism responding to dramatic events might not be capable of engineering a similar volte-face; namely the embrace of British Euro membership after years of anti-Euro rhetoric from the self-appointed representatives of Angleterre Profonde. As in July 1914 there is no political enthusiasm for European engagement at any level of any of the three main parties. A collective Euro-indifference worn at times heavily on the sleeve extends its deadening embrace cutting across all party lines. Nevertheless imagination suggests that it is not impossible for such studied indifference across the parties to change.

The Icelandic experience is salutary. Within a few weeks a profoundly Euro-sceptic population bludgeoned by events and humiliation shifted from undiluted hostility towards the Euro to enthusiasm. This brutal pattern of events could be repeated in the UK and certainly Sterling's imminent parity with the Euro is more than just the "correction from a rate between 1997 and 2007 which looked unsustainable".

However forcefully economists might argue that this devaluation is part of the "solution" to Britain's problems the fact remains that for hundreds of thousands of Britons with second homes in the Euro zone, notably France, Spain and Malta, devaluation is eroding living standards at a rate not experienced since the successive devaluations of the Labour governments in the late sixties. Then only a small minority which travelled to Europe was affected. Today the numbers directly impacted are immensely greater.

Nevertheless the pain experienced here is only part of the equation. Another factor is the perceived competence of the Bank of England. A series of misjudgements is creating a situation where there is an increasing danger that valid criticism becomes overtaken by the perception that the nation's financial well-being is somehow being put at risk by the Bank's disappointing failure to gauge the downside risks to UK activity and set interest rates accordingly. Rather belatedly the Bank has come to the conclusion that what it once regarded as improbable is indeed coming to pass. This misjudgement comes on the heels of earlier mistakes notably over Northern Rock. If the economists are prepared to break ranks and accuse the Bank of over elaborate forecasting models which muddy thinking, the man in the street despite his less exalted position can point to a string of events which at the very least place a serious question mark over this prestigious British institution's judgement.

Nowhere is this more apparent in that touchstone of wealth for the majority of English people: property prices. The Bank clearly misread the signal conveyed by collapsing house prices and has, mirabile dictu, come to the conclusion that house prices do not matter all that much for consumers' spending. This is a cardinal error the consequences of which may well come back to haunt the Bank and not least question its right to independence as the recession deepens.

This brings us to perhaps the greatest obstacle to British Euro-membership and certainly one which politicians fear most of all: the bar of public opinion. At present a referendum held on Euro membership would offer little guarantee of success for the pro-Euro cause. The media is overwhelmingly against it we are repeatedly told but it is not newspaper editors who "need to be bribed" — these are, as the events of the last few years vividly show, with one or two exceptions expendable individuals – it is their proprietors who must be persuaded. And here the recession provides a powerful weapon; as all newspapers face increasing pressure on their revenue they are open to any sound argument which would give their financing added stability.

The keystone to UK media Euro-scepticism remains the Murdoch owned press. Rupert Murdoch has made no secret of his hostility to the Euro and his newspapers including the mid-market Times and Sunday Times and the formidable "Sun" remain solidly subservient to this almost personal vendetta against Europe. Within five years however the Murdoch Empire will be embroiled in succession issues which will at the very least dilute the focus of this hostility. An agreement giving equal economic rights in the Murdoch family's stake in the company to all six of its chairman's children but voting control to the eldest four only, containing no provision for breaking tied votes would seem to foreshadow first the eclipse and then break-up of the once powerful empire. If the economic situation is deteriorating at the same time it is hard to see how implacable hostility towards the Euro will remain a priority for an organisation whose challenges will come from an entirely different direction.

As even the most articulate critics of Euro membership admit, the fiscal solvency of the UK cannot any longer be taken for granted. Though it is hard to see at present when UK gilts show no sign of an interest rate or currency risk premium how UK membership of the Euro could strengthen our fiscal position --- the Euro zone is after all explicitly not a fiscal union --- it is not impossible to see how membership of the Euro would encourage the UK to save more.

The momentum which is building up now for re-examining all these issues regrettably is a full-blown Sterling crisis; some would quip the traditional British way of ejecting a Labour government which has outstayed its welcome. Such a crisis is now more likely today than at any time in the last twenty years and will result in a destruction of British assets unrivalled since the late sixties. Inflation will be the inevitable corollary of a flight from sterling. In its wake the overwhelming mood of the country will be desperate for stability. A nostalgia even for the certainties of the Maastricht criteria and a deficit below 3% rather than the UK's current 8.1% may even become widespread. In such circumstances it is hard to see how stability can be attained except through union with a stronger currency.

It is not to be excluded that faced with crisis, the Euro-sceptics become vociferous proponents of currency union with the dollar; after all at least one proprietor of the Daily Telegraph now languishing behind bars frequently called for stronger ties with the North Atlantic. This old idea has been mooted before and will no doubt be raised again. But it will fail for the reason that it was rejected in the past: the price for the UK is too high.

Richard Bassett - Formerly Times Correspondent for Central and Eastern Europe. Executive Director Corporate Communications, WestLB AG. Author of recent much acclaimed biography of Admiral Wilhelm Canaris.

Time to Look Beyond the Five Tests?

UK based economists venturing across the channel are often perplexed to be asked when Britain is likely to join the Euro, and will, in turn, induce perplexity in their interlocutors by revealing that joining is simply not under discussion and has not been since being rejected more than five years ago. Yet in the current febrile economic environment, maybe it is time for the Brits not only to revisit the issue, but also (and more importantly) to ask whether the right questions are being posed in assessing the case for membership.

For most of the big decisions about the furthering of economic integration in Europe, the UK has been reluctant to jump in early, preferring instead to wait until there is compelling evidence that there will be net economic gains. The UK's position on EMU is very much in this tradition and extends the philosophy of waiting 'until the time is ripe' that was already adopted for earlier steps towards European monetary integration. Even the short-lived UK membership of the exchange rate mechanism (ERM) only occurred more than a decade after the system was launched.

Obstacles to declaring the time to be ripe have varied over the years. Britain's status as an oil exporter was especially prominent in the 1980s and into the 1990s, and the distinctive post-industrial character of the British economy has also been stressed. Other reasons put forward include the fact that Britain's mortgages are predominantly variable rate as opposed to fixed rate in the euro area, distinctive trade patterns and specialisations, and the suggestion that foreign investment from outside the Euro could be affected.

The five tests set out in 1997 by the then Chancellor, Gordon Brown, constitute a methodology for assessing whether or not the benefits of Euro membership exceed the costs sufficiently to justify joining. Although, at the time, their primary political purpose was to quarantine an issue that has so often been toxic in British politics and could have been damaging for the newly elected Labour government, they nevertheless offered a credible means of appraising the case for membership. Indeed, it is instructive that when a decision to stay out was taken in 2003, it was based on research that included 19 volumes of research and analysis, providing an empirical basis for the debate.

However, the five tests framework offers only an incomplete means of evaluating the case. Essentially, they apply a cost-benefit analysis approach to working out whether the UK and its prospective euro area partners would approximate to an optimal currency area. Thus, the convergence test examines whether the UK would gain or lose from a one-size-fits-all monetary policy, implicitly testing whether the shocks likely to hit the UK economy differ from those affecting its partners. Similarly, the flexibility and investment tests consider whether the economy is sufficiently able to adjust in the absence of exchange rate changes and independent monetary policy. In effect these tests are about the comparability of the structures of the economies that form a currency union.

While the five tests offer a crude, but not unreasonable means of assessing the costs and benefits for the real economy, they overlook a number of equally significant factors, especially the connection between the currency regime and financial stability. Over the last two decades, the changing fashions in monetary policy have placed price stabilisation ahead of financial stability in the priorities of central banks. The credit crunch has brutally exposed the shortcomings in this approach and is prompting a fresh look at the mix of policy objectives. It has also highlighted the speed with which financial contagion can spread and the tsunami-like character of the shock waves. And it has also shown that the major central banks have to act together to contain the threats to stability.

The establishment of the Euro has, on the whole, made it easier to deal with these problems, suggesting that in stormy weather it is helpful to have a safe haven. Consider how much more tricky it would have been to react to the financial crisis if Spain, Italy, France and Germany had been pursuing competitive macroeconomic and exchange rate strategies.

The arrangements for wider economic policy co-ordination are also part of the story. Although Keynes has been disinterred, orchestrating a common European approach in which the euro area and the UK adopt broadly similar packages to stimulate the economy remains difficult. Certainly, the evident tensions between France and Germany about how to proceed show that the mere fact of the Euro does not solve all problems. But the maturing institutions of euro area governance at least offer a framework for decision-making to which the UK has access only as a guest.

Moreover, in a post credit crunch world, regulatory reforms that focus on financial stability will have to be undertaken and their progress monitored. This, in turn, will require new governance structures, including a fresh look at how European countries are represented in international fora such as the IMF and any putative new bodies charged with oversight of the regulatory machinery. The tricky question the UK faces is whether its voice would be heard if it remains independent rather than being part of a wider euro grouping.

How then should the UK decide on the Euro? The public will still need to be persuaded that the net effect on the real economy will be favourable. However, the five tests were always imprecise and arriving at the 'clear and unambiguous' result Gordon Brown sought in setting up the tests was always going to be a matter of judgement as well as empirical economics. Even in today's volatile economic circumstances, an assessment of the tests could go either way depending on assumptions made and, let's be blunt, the political result that is wanted.

What should, though, become more pivotal in judging whether it is now in Britain's interest to join the Euro is the likely impact on financial stability and whether the new risks the economy faces can be adequately managed while the UK stands alone. Here the questions are beguilingly simple. First, would it be easier to deal with further problems affecting major financial intermediaries from within or outside the euro area? Second, if more active and co-ordinated macroeconomic policy-making is one outcome of the credit crisis, can it be achieved more easily by the UK joining the Euro or staying independent?

Larger and more diversified economies have a number of advantages in dealing with financial risks and turmoil. First, the economy will tend to be less specialised in financial services, with the result that the ratio of outstanding debt to GDP will be lower. Iceland is an extreme case and Switzerland also has a high ratio. In good times, Iceland benefited from the activities of its banks in external markets, but when the crisis hit it rapidly became apparent that it was not just the banks, but the country as a whole that was in default. By contrast, Luxembourg or Ireland (both of which have become relatively specialised in financial services), have the rest of the euro area as a source of liquidity.

Second, a large economy has the financial muscle to act decisively. Indeed, there is a close parallel between the notion of a bank that is too big to fail and an economy that is too big to fail. A bankrupt Latin American country is an inconvenience and, apart from the embarrassment of a few local authority treasurers, the meltdown of a tiny economy like Iceland has few ramifications, but a default by the euro area is inconceivable. The UK is still a large economy and financial problems would have to worsen by an order of magnitude before British government-backed loans became junk, but a perception of vulnerability could result in a worsening of terms with adverse long-run consequences. Third, large economies can shape the global response to the sort of financial instability that has surfaced over the last eighteen months, whether through leading concerted action or through instigating reforms of the system.

Do financial stability and economic governance considerations trump the optimal currency area reasoning behind the five tests? Some commentators, such as the distinguished *Financial Times* columnist Martin Wolf, have argued that the UK needs exchange rate and interest rate flexibility more than ever to deal with the fallout from the credit crisis. But a forceful counter-argument is that the real remedy will come from co-ordinated international action to shore up bank balance sheets and to maintain aggregate demand. A country such as the UK may gain temporary respite by devaluation, but only by what is in effective a protectionist device to gain market share and by risking longer-term inflation. Moreover, it is not through devaluation that the health of the banking system will be restored, but by policies that assure an appropriate balance between risk and solidity.

The conclusion to draw is that the old approaches to assessing Euro membership are past their sell-by dates, and that the decision now has to pay far more heed to financial stability and the position of the UK in the governance of the international financial system. By these latter criteria, the case for the UK to think afresh looks different and stronger.

Iain Begg - Professorial Research Fellow, European Institute, LSE.

Britain's Eternal Vulnerability: Sterling

This paper is designed to help answer three simple questions that UK citizens should have asked some time ago – and will certainly be demanding answers by the time of the next General Election. Future generations of historians will argue about the details for decades to come but some simple facts are now speaking loudly for themselves. But this author has no doubt that Britain stands at an economic cross-roads – after a decade of economic stewardship by one man.

1. Why has Sterling fallen so much in the last 15 months?
2. Does it matter?
3. What can be done about sterling?

Graham Bishop

The value of sterling is a useful barometer of what the rest of the world thinks about the sustainability of the United Kingdom's economic policies. The magnitude of the 27% decline against a broad basket of currencies since summer 2007 is a dramatic statement by the foreigners.

If the exchange rate does not rebound substantially and quickly from current levels, then the devaluation since 2007 will rival that of 1931/32, when Britain came off the Gold Standard - a period etched into Britain's economic history. It was associated with such severe economic problems that the conversion of 5% War Loan 1929/32 (amounting to 40% of GDP in a single bond) to 3.5% War Loan 1952/onwards was effectively a default on our public debt as that bond is still outstanding and the inflation-adjusted value has been eroded to virtually zero.

Annual averages may smooth out fluctuations and give a better feel for the impact on trade but can also obscure step changes. The most profound was the 30% devaluation in 1949. **At the current rate of €0.95/£, the decline over the past 18 months now matches the devaluation that marked the effective end of Britain's economic and political super-power status.**

Figure 1
Sterling devaluations in the past 100 years: % depreciation of annual average rate versus US dollar

Period	1919/20	1931/32	1979/50	1967/68	1975/76	2007/08
Devaluation	-17%	-28%	-24%	-15%	-22%	-13%

Sources: The Economist, 100 Years of Economic Statistics; Bank of England

So the foreign holders of sterling are sending Britain a message with a force that has only been witnessed a handful of times in the last 100 years. **Astonishingly, Britain's political class seems not to have heard, let alone grasped, the profound implications.** Perhaps they are simply "in denial". Certainly there is no discussion about what should be done – and now even more importantly, what **can** be done.

The idea of joining the Euro is dismissed outright on the basis that we would not qualify – judged on the Maastricht criteria. But the instant dismissal starts from the rejection of the political implications for the Labour Party having to admit the failure of its economic stewardship for a decade. The Official Opposition – the Conservative Party – is perhaps determined to avoid confronting the demon that tore it apart in the 1990's – Europe.

Meeting the Maastricht criteria

Examining the European Commission's October 2008 forecasts for 2009 suggests that the UK would still meet the public debt criterion – but probably not in 2010. The UK would easily fulfil the inflation test – 1.9% versus the average of 1.9% for the three best performing EU members (Sweden, France and Spain/Austria). So the 1.5 percentage points of leeway versus these states would not have to be used at all. The long-term interest rate criterion versus those states' bonds is also met very comfortably. But the UK ostensibly fails two vital criteria: the budget deficit is likely to be three times the limit and it would be difficult to say that sterling is stable – whether in the ERM or not.

But that is the conventional economists' reading of the Maastricht Treaty text. Importantly, the authors left the political leaders some flexibility. The reports on the economic numbers will be drawn up by the European Commission and Central Bank in accordance with the formulae but the Finance Ministers only use them as "the basis" for their "assessment" of whether an "excessive deficit" exists on the basis of "planned" deficits. That assessment is passed to the Heads of Government who then "confirm which Member States fulfil the necessary conditions for the adoption of the single currency."

Why might the political leaders of the Eurozone be persuaded to take such a risk? They may now be looking nervously at the economic implications for their own countries of this massive sterling devaluation.

So a major recession in Britain is manifestly bad for the volume of the Eurozone's exports, but the real nightmare would be unparalleled cost competitiveness in third country markets. Based on current exchange rates, the UK's competitiveness is now at about 74 versus the Eurozone 15 or EU 27 – matching the extreme cost competitiveness of the mid 1990's (see Figure 2).

Unit labour costs for the whole British economy have exceeded the Eurozone average by 1.4% annually between 1997 and 2006, but have slowed to about the same as the Eurozone since. This explains the steady loss of competitiveness that has progressively manifested itself in the growing current account deficit. So it would be easy to argue that the first phase of sterling weakness to say mid-2008 was just a necessary offsetting of this lost competitiveness.

But the recent collapse may mark an altogether more ominous phase if it is not reversed quickly. That would be the moment when Britain's problem became the Eurozone's problem, and potentially a fundamental challenge to the European Union's entire concept of a single market for goods and services. A blatantly competitive devaluation might not be seen by the other players as "cricket".

Figure 2
Relative cost indicators, based on
unit labour costs in total economy

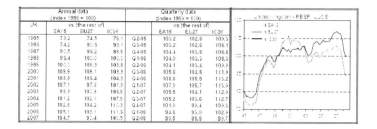

Annual data (index 1999 = 100)			Quarterly data (index 1999 = 100)			
UK vs (the rest of)				vs (the rest of)		
EA15	EU27	IC36		EA15	EU27	IC36
73.2	74.5	79.1	Q2-05	105.2	102.6	109.5
74.2	80.6	93.1	Q3-05	105.2	102.6	108.1
90.5	96.2	98.9	Q4-05	104.4	103.8	108.6
96.4	100.0	100.0	Q1-06	104.0	103.5	108.3
100.0	100.3	100.3	Q2-06	104.1	103.4	109.9
109.9	108.1	103.3	Q3-06	105.8	104.8	111.9
108.8	105.4	104.3	Q4-06	106.6	105.5	115.2
107.1	97.8	101.3	Q1-07	107.0	105.7	115.9
99.3	100.8	105.9	Q2-07	105.5	104.1	112.9
101.2	102.1	107.9	Q3-07	105.2	103.6	112.7
102.8	104.2	110.3	Q4-07	101.0	99.4	109.5
105.1	103.1	111.5	Q1-08	94.6	93.0	102.9
104.7	97.4	100.5	Q2-08	90.5	88.9	99.7

Source: European Commission, Cost and Price Competitiveness, 2Q 2008

What is the foreigner's risk/reward trade-off in holding sterling assets, or even buying more?

This is the key to sterling's precipitate decline: steadily rising current account deficits have accumulated to an uncomfortable degree of indebtedness and the sustainability of fiscal policy is now being questioned. In current terminology, this combination is seen as "toxic".

Buyers and sellers of sterling

The UK's current account deficit is likely to improve somewhat as the decline in sterling improves our competitiveness – but there will be the usual J-curve effects to surmount first. Moreover, a synchronised global downturn means that export demand will be depressed almost whatever the exchange rate. So it could be a year or two before the UK's current account deficit swings round into surplus. Indeed, the Treasury's December survey of independent forecasters shows that the newly-published forecasts for 2009 still show an average expectation of a £38 billion current account deficit – exactly the same as in 2008.

In 2009 alone, we will continue to need the foreigner to be willing to finance **extra** sterling balances of about 3% of GDP.

By contrast, the euro area's traditional small surplus in its current account has now eased back to balance. **So foreign holders of sterling rather than Euro are confronted by the question of stabilising the counterpart £265 billion (19% of GDP) debt incurred to them in the last decade. This was funded by just £15 billion of capital account inflows and a massive £255 billion of financial inflows (according to the 2008 Pink Book of the UK's Balance of Payments).**

But these net inflows are the balance of truly dramatic gross flows. In 2007, inflows were £1020 <u>billion</u> (of which £743 billion were "other") and outflows were £981 <u>billion</u> (of which £733 were "other"). The colossal scale of these flows – much more than our GDP – illustrates the scale of the City of London's role as a global financial centre and especially as the financial centre of the Eurozone. So a small change in these gross flows could have a dramatic impact at the net level.

Operators of these flows may be comforted by the size of Britain's "Official Holdings of International Reserves". At the end of November, 2008, these amounted to $52.4 billion. But that is the gross figure and netting off the liabilities reduced the total to $26.5 billion. Some of that is illiquid gold (after being halved by Chancellor Brown in earlier years). Some is represented by various tranches of Special Drawing Rights (SDRs) at the IMF. Any hint of conditionality in their use is likely to remind a Labour Chancellor of the humiliation of Chancellor Healey in 1976. (He had to turn back from a foreign trip when he had only got as far as Heathrow Airport so that he could negotiate an emergency loan from the IMF.)

So the immediately useable portion of these reserves may be no more than the "Bank of England Foreign Currency Assets and Liabilities". At the end of November 2008, these amounted to $12.6 billion **gross**, or just a paltry $4 billion of **net** assets. This would explain the UK's steadfast policy of non-intervention during recent periods of volatile trading.

Buyers and seller of UK government bonds

The UK's public finances have deteriorated dramatically with the structural deficit likely to be 40% higher over the 5 years to 2010. The contrast with the Eurozone is again sharp: "they" realised they were not meeting their own commitments in 2004 and revised the Stability and Growth Pact (SGP) – signed by Chancellor Brown - as an EU-wide commitment. The Eurozone took it seriously and cut their cyclically-adjusted deficit from 2.7% of GDP in 2004 to 1.2% by 2007. It seems likely to edge up to a 1.4% for the next couple of years.

Figure 3
Euro area fiscal developments
(general government as % of GDP)

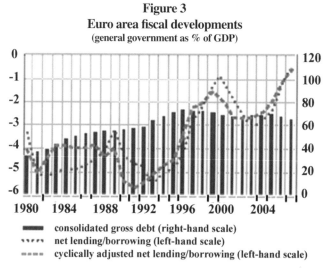

▬▬▬	consolidated gross debt (right-hand scale)
▼▼▼▼	net lending/borrowing (left-hand scale)
═══	cyclically adjusted net lending/borrowing (left-hand scale)

Sources: The European Commission's AMECO database and ECB calculations.
Note: Data exclude receipts from the sale of Universal Mobile Telecommunication System (UMTS) licences.
1) Potential GDP as estimated by the European Commission.

The UK response to its renewed commitment was to bring that measure of the deficit down from 3.7% to 3.0% by 2006. Since then it has moved in the opposite direction to the Eurozone. Historians may record this as the fatal policy error because the deficit has risen by half and already seems likely to double from the low point by 2010. Such Commission calculations were before the new expansion of the deficit set out in the PBR. **The**

sustainability, let alone the credibility, of British fiscal policy is now being seriously questioned – with good reason.

Budget deficits have to be financed – either from domestic savings or from foreign inflows (assuming that the Bank of England's banknote printing works at Debden will not be compelled to work overtime!). The Treasury's December survey of independent economists revealed an average deficit forecast of £117 billion for the year starting April 2009. Subsequent data already suggests the outturn will be even higher.

The first line of funding is from the long term savings institutions such as pension funds and life insurance etc. In 2006, their total investments in <u>all</u> types of assets were £74 billion and that rose to £92 billion in 2007. Remarkably, the provisional estimates show only £1.4 billion net investments in the first half of 2008.

Even if all private sector investment were entirely crowded out, there may still be a shortfall exceeding £30 billion. If this were financed by the banking system, then such loans would not be made to risky SMEs, residential mortgages etc. These are precisely the sectors that are allegedly starved of new loans and thus exacerbating the economic downturn. The UK seems close to a vicious spiral in its public finances, given the high leverage of the public deficit to even a modest downturn in activity. **This risk matters enormously to the citizens of the UK.**

The impact of sterling

This is the point where the outlook for sterling impinges decisively on the debate: At short maturities, the foreigner now earns less on sterling than on Euros and interest rate futures completely discount sterling and Euro rates remaining very similar throughout 2009, with many commentators calling for additional cuts – even to 0%.

With no relative reward and sharply rising fiscal riskiness, it is very easy to understand why the foreigner wishes to reduce

exposure to sterling assets. Is there a natural floor for sterling? Not during a global slowdown as export markets may not respond easily to the new competitiveness. A continuing large current account deficit requires foreigners to keep net buying of sterling financial assets running at £40 billion annually. If they do not do this, then effectively UK consumers will be selling sterling day in and day out.

Note: There is an interesting comparison with non-Eurozone member Denmark. In the early years of this century, the current account **surplus** *averaged 3-4% of GDP, leading to gross reserves of foreign currency of around €22 billion (nearly 70% larger than those of the UK); the cyclically-adjusted budget* **surplus** *was 3.7% of GDP in 2007 so it has room for a reduction to perhaps 1.5% of GDP by 2010. The actual budget* **surplus** *is likely to decline from around 4.5% of GDP to under 1% in the next couple of years. So debt levels have fallen continuously this century and are likely to stabilise at about 20% of GDP – one-third of the UK's prospective levels.*

So the foreigner was looking at an incomparably stronger position than that of Britain. Nonetheless, recently Denmark faced some downward pressure on its currency and found it necessary to raise interest rates to a 25% premium relative to Euro rates after it lost nearly half its foreign exchange reserves in October (before replenishing them with borrowings). As the realisation sinks in to Danish society that there is a significant cost to being outside the Eurozone even with such robust finances, there is likely to be a referendum during 2009 on joining it.

What can be done?

Given the insufficiency of domestic savings and the imminent risk of a spiralling crowding out of private sector credit demands, the role of foreign inflows is vital. At the very least, they must be persuaded that there is enough investment attraction to finance the continuing current account deficit. If they judge the stance of fiscal policy to be unsustainable, then they are unlikely to make that investment. So the first task should be to restore the credibility of fiscal policy during this downturn.

The G20 communiqué put this succinctly: "Use fiscal measures to stimulate domestic demand to rapid effect, **as appropriate**, while maintaining a **policy framework conducive to fiscal sustainability**." *[emboldened statements are the author's emphasis as this wording seems to imply clearly that countries with serious fiscal problems should consider the sustainability of their position first. As Britain now faces a budget deficit probably three times the EU's recommended maximum (as accepted by the UK in 2005), it is hard to reconcile our signature on the G20 communiqué with the PBR actions]*

After a decade of promises that have been ignored or repudiated at the first sign of awkward times, it is difficult to see that the rest of the world will view internal UK commitments as credible. So the solution to the sterling crisis may well involve external oversight of the UK's public finances. Will a Labour Government turn to the IMF again as it did in 1976? Does the IMF even have the resources to fund the initial balance of payments deficit and also provide a standby facility that is large enough to convince the £250ish billion of foreign holders of sterling financial assets that it is sensible to remain? The major UK financial institutions also need to be sufficiently convinced that they do not feel it prudent to put a few more percentage points of their £3000 billion of clients' financial assets abroad.

Under these circumstances, the creation of an anchor for sterling may require the certainty that this will never happen again. That would point to the abolition of sterling and its replacement by a currency that has already established a solid track record – the Euro. The UK would have to convince the political leaders of the rest of Europe that their "planned" fiscal policy was indeed credible as it moved towards that of the rest of the Eurozone.

So that would be the point where the EU's political leaders would have an awkward decision to contemplate. The conventional, economist's reading of the Maastricht Treaty text may have to be supplemented by political realism as the leaders consider the impact of a seriously competitive devaluation by one of the biggest players in Europe's single market.

Graham Bishop - Former Director of Salomon Brothers. Adviser on the deregulation of European financial markets due to the Single Market programme and monetary union to the European Parliament and Commission and to committees of the House of Commons and the House of Lords.

The Overwhelming Economic Case for the United Kingdom Adopting the Euro

Introduction

It is time to revisit the 'Five Tests', to declare them passed and, subject to the UK being deemed, by our EU partners, to meet the Maastricht criteria, for the UK to adopt the Euro. Remember the 'Five Tests' designed at the behest of then Chancellor Gordon Brown? Passing these economic tests was presented as a necessary condition for the UK to apply for full membership in the Economic and Monetary Union (EMU).

For those who don't remember the Five Tests, here they are again:

1. Are business cycles and economic structures compatible so that we and others could live comfortably with Euro interest rates on a permanent basis?

2. If problems emerge is there sufficient flexibility to deal with them?

3. Would joining EMU create better conditions for firms making long-term decisions to invest in Britain?

4. What impact would entry into EMU have on the competitive position of the UK's financial services industry, particularly the City's wholesale markets?

5. In summary, will joining EMU promote higher growth, stability and a lasting increase in jobs?

The UK Treasury was given the task of assessing the tests - independently and without any regard to the political preferences of the political leadership, of course. The first assessment was in October 1997. The Treasury concluded that the UK economy was neither sufficiently converged with that of the rest of the EU, nor sufficiently flexible to apply for membership. Thus was a golden opportunity missed for the UK to become a full member of the EMU and thereby to benefit from the greater degree of macroeconomic and financial stability made possible by participation in the world's largest monetary union.

The second and thus far last assessment was published in 2003. The verdict of the Treasury was: closer but no cigar. Specifically:

- There had been significant progress on cyclical convergence since 1997, but significant structural differences remained, especially in the housing market.

- UK flexibility had improved (it had to, after six years of New Labour). The Treasury could not be certain, however, that the improvement had been sufficient.

- Investment would increase as a result of Euro area membership if and only if there had been sufficient convergence and flexibility.

- The City of London (accounting for roughly four percent of UK GDP, out of a total financial services sector of around 9 percent of GDP) would benefit from Euro area membership.

- As regards growth, stability and employment, see the third bullet point.

I have decided to save the Treasury (who have more urgent things on their mind right now) the time and effort of making another assessment by doing it myself. It should be clear from the Treasury's own 2003 assessment, that the third test (investment) and the fifth test (growth, stability employment) would be satisfied if and only if the other three are satisfied. I shall therefore just consider the first, second and fourth tests.

The main new finding of this paper is that the global financial crisis that started in August 2007 provides yet another powerful and sufficient argument for the UK to join the EMU and adopt the Euro as soon as technically possible. This new financial stability argument for UK membership in the EMU (which implies that the fourth test has been passed) is separate from and in addition to the conventional optimal currency arguments for joining (which correspond to the first two tests), which have also become more persuasive in the past few years.

1. Conventional arguments for the UK joining the Eurozone

These conventional arguments – (1) the incidence of asymmetric shocks or the asymmetric transmission of common shocks (cyclical convergence), (2) the degree of labour market and product market flexibility of and international factor mobility and (3) the ability to use fiscal policy in a countercyclical fashion - all point firmly towards EMU membership as the optimal UK monetary and exchange rate regime as well. The opportunity cost of a common currency – the loss of national monetary policy, that is, of the nominal exchange rate and/or the short-term risk-free nominal interest rate as possible policy instruments – is likely to be negative for the UK.

(1) Convergence

As regards cyclical convergence, the UK business cycle is now so synchronised with that of the Eurozone that the country looks like a suburb of Frankfurt. Chart 1 makes this clear using the monthly Total Economy Purchasing Managers Index (PMI) for the UK and Eurozone. The degree of convergence has been high since the Euro was created in 1999. In the last few years, including during the current recession, it has become astonishing. We should also keep in mind the endogeneity of the optimal currency area ((OCA) criteria: independent monetary policy can be a cause of cyclical divergence (see Frankel and Rose (1998)).

Chart 1

Cyclical Convergence UK and Euro zone 1998.06 - 2008.10
PMI Total Economy. SA 50+ = expansion average

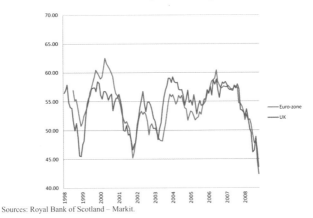

Sources: Royal Bank of Scotland – Markit.

A special dimension of *structural* asymmetry between the UK and the Eurozone often brought up as an obstacle to monetary union is the housing market. The UK is alleged to have a higher degree of home ownership than the Eurozone. Much UK residential mortgage financing is at variable rates, while more Eurozone residential mortgage financing is at fixed rates. Most of this is myth. UK owner-occupancy rates are not exceptionally high among European nations, as is clear from Table 1.

Table 1

Owner-occupancy rates in selected EU countries 2007

UK	Germany	Italy	Netherlands	Spain	Sweden	France
67%	41%	78%	50%	78%	61%	54%

Sources: Halifax

Moreover, the implication of whatever structural differences exist between the housing markets for the desirability of an independent monetary policy is less than obvious. Martin Wolf often stresses the fact that 'interest rates' in the Eurozone have been below those in the UK, and that without those higher UK interest rates, things would have been much worse for the UK (see Wolf (2008)). Chart 2 shows that he is correct in this assertion as regards short-term nominal interest rates, at least till November 2008.[1]

Chart 2

Short-term interest rates in Euro zone and UK 1990.01 - 2008.09

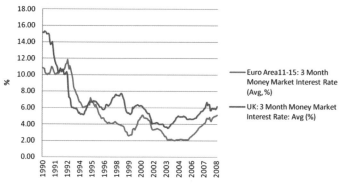

Source: Statistical Office of the European Communities

---

[1]   Eurozone data before 1999 are for a synthetic 11-country Eurozone.

The most recent, December 2008, Bank Rate is, at 2.00 percent, below the ECB's 2.50 percent main refinancing operations Fixed rate. This reversal of the historical pattern for short-term rates started in November 2008. In addition, Charts 3 and 4 demonstrate that long-term nominal interest rates and long-term real interest rates in the UK and in the Eurozone have been closely aligned since at least the beginning of the decade. Long-term rates are arguably more important drivers of aggregate demand than short-term nominal rates in both the UK and in the Eurozone.

Chart 3
Long-term interest rates in Euro zone and UK 1990.01 - 2008.09

Source: DG II/Statistical Office of the European Communities

Chart 4

Long-term real interest rates in Euro zone and UK 1994.01 - 2008.10

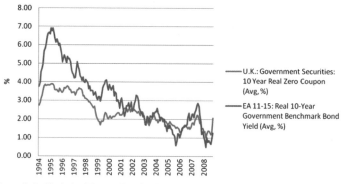

Source: Bank of England and European Central Bank

I would emphasize that the judgement that the UK needed (needs?) systematically higher short-term nominal interest rates than the Eurozone to keep the housing market from running amok is not convincing. Higher UK short-term nominal interest rates did not prevent the out-of-control housing finance boom and house price bubble that preceded the house price decline and home lending crash that started at the end of 2007.

The UK model of housing finance is broken. Measures to encourage truly long-term fixed-rate financing (20-year or 30-year fixed rate mortgages) are long overdue. New mortgage financing has collapsed, the securitisation of new mortgages has ground to a halt, and the construction sector (residential and commercial) is teetering on the brink of disaster. The culprit was ineffective UK regulation, not just of residential mortgage finance but of household borrowing and of the financial sector generally. One indicator of the loss of financial control in the UK is that the UK household sector is the most leveraged in the developed world.[2]

---

2   The UK's ratio of household debt to annual household disposable income at the end of 2007 was 170 percent. In the US the corresponding figure was 140 percent; in the Eurozone it was 100 percent.

In the Eurozone too there are countries that have dysfunctional housing finance, household sector financing and indeed discredited regulatory regimes for the financial sector as a whole. Ireland is one example. Spain, with its unprecedented almost two decades-long construction boom/bubble is another example. But there are also examples of superior continental models of housing finance and of financial regulation in general. The Netherlands and France provide superior templates, in my view. The current crisis and collapse of the UK residential mortgage financing system provide an ideal opportunity to redesign the system along best-practice European lines.

(2) **Flexibility**.

The UK economy's main product markets and labour markets are at least as flexible as their Eurozone counterparts. Since 2004, there has been a further major enhancement in the UK's ability to respond to any asymmetric shocks through the large-scale equilibrating flows of labour between the new EU member states in Eastern and Central Europe (especially Poland) and the UK. CEE workers came in their hundreds of thousands when the UK economy was booming. They are leaving in their hundreds of thousands now that the economy is collapsing. Chart 5 shows the step-up in gross and net immigration into the UK in 2004. The ONS estimates that 96,000 Polish citizens migrated into the UK in 2007 (the last boom year), which was the highest inflow of any individual citizenship.

Chart 5

Total International Migration to and from the UK 1998 - 2007

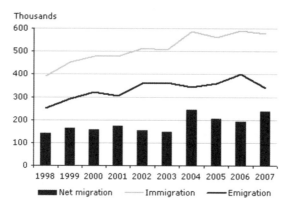

Source: Office for National Statistics, National Statistics Online.

(3) Fiscal policy

The Stability and Growth Pact currently applies formally in a slightly weaker form to countries that have an opt-out from EMU (the UK and Denmark): the financial sanctions that can in principle be imposed on persistent SGP transgressors, cannot be imposed on the opt-outs. As it is clear that even for full EMU members, the threat of financial sanctions being imposed on those who offend the letter and spirit of the SGP is not credible, the UK has no reason to fear that joining the Eurozone will lead to a reduction in its ability to use fiscal policy freely to manage its national economy. Eurozone member states are certainly pulling out the stops at least as radically as the UK when it comes to Keynesian deficit financing to mitigate the collapse of private effective demand.

Even for the full EMU members, the SGP has not been a meaningful constraint on national fiscal discretion. We have seen this during the boom periods, when pro-cyclical fiscal policy was the rule. We are seeing it now during the downturn, when it is clear that no country will run into any form of trouble from Brussels for exceeding the three percent of GDP limit for the general government financial deficit. Exceptional circumstances require exceptional measures. An exceptional downturn requires large increases in government deficits. For better or worse, the SGP is not and will not be a binding constraint on national budgetary policies.

(4) The fine-tuning fallacy - the illusion that independent national monetary policy can be used to respond effectively to asymmetric shocks.

The argument that the UK would suffer as the result of the loss of national monetary sovereignty and its replacement by a one-size-fits-all official policy rate and common external bilateral exchange rates, stands or falls with the usefulness of national monetary policy as a stabilisation tool. I have argued for the best part of a decade, that a small open economy like the UK, with a floating exchange rate and a very high degree of international capital mobility, is better off as a member of a larger currency union, even if it is faced with asymmetric shocks (Buiter(1999a,b, 2000, 2008a)).

There is quite a lot of evidence to support the view, that a floating exchange rate under conditions of high international capital mobility is not a shock-absorber or a buffer that permits necessary changes in international relative costs and prices to be achieved through costless changes in the nominal exchange rate rather than through painful changes in relative domestic and foreign nominal costs and prices – painful especially for those countries that have to reduce the rate of inflation or perhaps even the level of their home currency costs and prices.

Instead a floating nominal exchange rate, when domestic costs and prices are sticky, is a source of extraneous noise, excess short-term volatility and persistent medium-term misalignments of and lasting distortions of international competitiveness when capital is highly mobile. The reason is that, far from being set at a level that puts international relative prices of goods, services and factors of production at their fundamental values, the exchange rate is determined/set proximately in asset markets. Like most other financial markets, the market for foreign exchange is, even when it is technically efficient in the sense of low transactions costs and few opportunities for profitable arbitrage, a highly inefficient pricing mechanism from the perspective of allocative efficiency. It reflects not just fundamentals (or people's view of fundamentals) but all the fears, phobias, hopes and impulses that drive foreign exchange traders and their principals. Bubbles, sudden mood swings from euphoria to despondency, from irrational exuberance to unwarranted depression, herding behaviour and bandwagon effects are the rule, not the exception.

Thus, a floating exchange rate under high international capital mobility is far from performing like an automatic stabiliser. It is even further from being an effective policy instrument. It is an outcome of uncontrolled and uncontrollable processes, many of which we don't understand and cannot predict, rather like a rogue elephant.

Even a gun fired at random by a drunk may, from time to time, hit the target. This is what we have seen in the UK with the exchange rate this past year. As shown in Chart 6, between its peak in 2007.01 and 2008.10, the broad effective exchange rate of sterling depreciated by 15.5 percent. Since then it may have fallen by another 12 percent or so, following the unexpected 150 basis points cut in Bank Rate in November 2008 and the further cut of 100 basis points in December 2008. This is good news for all those who try to produce things in the UK in competition with foreign producers. But this relief comes after a 10-year period of overvaluation, when sterling's nominal and real exchange rates were those of a country driven by the Dutch disease.

Chart 6
UK Exchange rates, US$, Euro and Effective 1975.01 - 2008.10

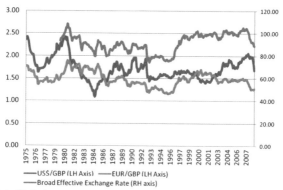

Source: Bank of England

With the benefit of hindsight, we now can see that this may indeed have been what was happening, with the increasingly bloated UK financial sector playing the role normally played by the resource-extracting sector and the government budget in the Dutch disease scenario. The ten years of damage to the real economy done by sterling's real misalignment was not mitigated by sterling's nominal flexibility. The collapse of the UK's financial sector since August 2007 represents the end of the financial-sector-driven Dutch disease episode for the UK. It is helpful that the nominal exchange rate has, for once, done the right thing by depreciating sharply, to permit other tradable sectors to attract resources. But this is not something that one can count on. It was not predicted by the policy makers or planned by them. It happened to them. In the case of the US, where a further real exchange rate depreciation is necessary to undo systemic external imbalances, the exchange rate has gone the wrong way since last summer, driven by ephemeral short-run financial rather than by long-term fundamentals.

Even in a rather closed continent-sized economy like the US or the Eurozone, monetary policy works with lags that are often long and always variable and uncertain. In a small open economy like the UK, where much of the transmission of monetary policy is through the exchange rate, the uncertainty about the timing, the magnitude and sometimes even the direction of the effects of monetary policy and other shocks on the exchange rate and other variables of interest is such that independent monetary policy is a curse, not a blessing. By joining a larger monetary union and thus reducing the exposure of the real economy to the financial casino that is the foreign exchange market, the macroeconomic stability of the UK economy will be enhanced.

(5) **Monetary union because of, not despite, asymmetric shocks**

One can quite easily stand the asymmetric shocks argument on its head: precisely when there are asymmetric shocks to national GDPs, a common currency is desirable. Even when policy cannot be used to dampen, let alone eliminate, these asymmetric GDP fluctuations, it may be possible to smooth national consumption over time and across states of nature through international portfolio diversification. International financial portfolio diversification decouples GDP (income generated within a given national jurisdiction) from GNP (income earned by residents of a given national jurisdiction). Together with taxation (net of transfers) and saving, it permits the decoupling of private consumption from GDP.

International portfolio diversification is limited by a number of factors. Currency risk is one of them, along with informational asymmetries, transaction costs, and investor sentiment. The creation of EMU has led to a significant reduction in 'home' bias in equity investment among the EMU members, although there remains a rather strong 'Euro bias' (see Giofré (2008)). By permitting or encouraging greater international portfolio diversification,

EMU contributes to economic stability according to the more relevant metric of consumption variability rather than GDP variability.

2. The financial stability argument for UK membership in the EMU

The argument that having an independent currency means increased financial instability for the UK does not depend on whether one agrees with my view that the Bank of England has, since August 2007, been the most inept of the leading central banks in the area of liquidity management - the art and science of providing illiquid financial enterprises and illiquid markets with, respectively, funding liquidity and market liquidity. After a dreadful start in August 2007, when the Bank insisted on following what amounted to a 'Treasuries only' collateral policy at its discount window (the standing lending facility) and in its repos, there were signs of real progress starting in the late autumn of 2007, culminating in the creation of the Special Liquidity Scheme (SLS).

Since then, it has all been downhill again, however. The SLS was restricted to asset-backed securities and covered bonds backed by 'old' mortgages and other underlying assets only - assets originated before December 31, 2007. This did nothing to revive the securitisation of new mortgages.

Instead of extending the SLS to new originations, the Bank announced last summer that it would close the existing SLS to new business by October 21, 2008. This created a prominent focal point for coordinating those wishing to short sell bank equity or to cut off credit lines to banks suspected of having significant amounts of SLS-type assets on their balance sheets. The demise of HBOS (Halifax-Bank of Scotland) as an independent institution can be traced directly to this most unfortunate announcement.

The Bank of England recognised its error and announced an extension of the deadline for new business at the SLS during the height of the banking panic that followed the announcement that Lehman Brothers had filed for bankruptcy protection on September 15, 2008. It once again specified a specific date for the end of new business, however – this time the end of January 2009. Once again, the Bank of England has created a perfect focal point for speculative attacks on banks holding (or suspected of holding) large amounts of illiquid assets. It is obvious that the terminal date of an arrangement like the SLS ought to be state-contingent rather than time-contingent: the SLS should be open for new business until, in the judgement of the authorities, the conditions necessitating its existence have vanished.

The Bank has also failed to address the widening of the spreads between the unsecured interbank lending rate (Libor) and the expected future official policy rate (as measured, say, by the overnight indexed swap rate (OIS). While Mervyn King is no doubt correct that the 5 to 20 basis points spreads we saw before the crisis between 3-month Libor and the 3-month OIS rate reflected irrational optimism and under-priced default risk, it seems equally clear to me that the 200-plus spreads we have seen since the middle of September 2008 overstate fundamental counterparty risk. Much more aggressive quantitative easing and qualitative easing will be necessary, especially now that Bank Rate is getting close to the zero lower bound.

Although it is regrettably true that the Bank of England too often has been part of the problem in the financial markets rather than part of the solution, and that the ECB has acquitted itself far better in that regard, this in itself is not the main reason why it would be desirable to get rid of sterling (see Buiter (2008b)). The financial stability case against sterling and for the Euro would exist even if the Bank's liquidity management and market support had been of the very highest quality.

In a nutshell, the argument goes as follows. There is no such thing as a safe bank, even if the bank is sound in the sense that, if it could hold its existing assets to maturity, it would be able to meet all its contractual obligations. More generally, there is no such thing as a safe highly leveraged institution that borrows short and lends/invests long and illiquid. Government guarantees/support are required to make private financial institutions with leverage and asset-liability mismatch sustainable. Such support is provided in the first instance by the central bank acting as lender of last resort and market maker of last resort (see Buiter (2008b)). This central bank must be backed by a fiscal authority with spare fiscal capacity (the capacity and willingness to raise the present discounted value of its future primary (non-interest) surpluses).

When the short-term liabilities of the banks are denominated in domestic currency, there is no limit to the amount of appropriate liquidity the central bank can provide - costlessly and instantaneously. It can simply create additional base money. The only constraints on its willingness to provide liquidity would be fear of moral hazard and fear of the inflation the monetary expansion might create. Moral hazard can be dealt with by pricing the liquidity support appropriately and by imposing regulatory requirements on entities borrowing from the central bank. The threat of inflation is present only if the borrowing banks turn out to be insolvent rather than just illiquid but solvent. In that case, if the solvency gap of the banks is sufficiently large, it may not be possible for the central bank to recapitalise the insolvent banks by creating money without driving inflation above its target level. To avoid excessive inflation, the Treasury will have to recapitalise the insolvent banks instead of the central bank.

When a significant share of the short-term liabilities of the banking system (broadly defined to include the AIGs, GEs and GMACs of this world) is denominated in foreign currency, there are limits to the foreign currency liquidity support the central bank can provide. Foreign exchange reserves, credit lines and swaps are small outside a small number of newly prominent emerging markets like China and some of the GCC states. For the UK they are negligible. The total amount of foreign exchange reserves of the UK (fiscal and monetary) authorities is around $50 billion.

So to act as a lender of last resort or market maker of last resort in foreign currency, the Bank of England would, in short order, have to approach the central banks of the only two countries/ regions that have serious global reserve currencies: the USA (the US dollar makes up around 64 percent of global reserves) and the Euro area (the Euro accounts for around 27 percent). No doubt it would be possible for the Bank of England to arrange swaps with the Fed and the ECB (if the UK Treasury were to back such a request), but there would be a cost.

This insurance premium for foreign exchange liquidity risk would make the City of London less competitive compared to institutions operating in the jurisdictions of the Fed and the ECB. Clearly, the solvency of the UK sovereign is the ultimate determinant of the ability of the central bank to borrow foreign exchange at any price. In the case of a request for access to additional foreign-currency liquidity, it must be credible that the authorities in the borrowing nation are capable of making both the internal fiscal transfer (from tax payers or from the current beneficiaries of public spending to the state) and the external transfer (from domestic to foreign residents) required to service the additional debt incurred by the state.

Given the size of the gross external liabilities of the UK (see Chart 7), many of which can be assumed to have short maturities, and given the size of the foreign currency liabilities of the UK banking sector (see Chart 8), which can safely be assumed to have shorter remaining maturities and to be more liquid than the foreign currency assets (it is banks we are dealing with!), the ability of the state to provide a credible guarantee for the survival of the UK banking sector cannot be taken for granted.

Chart 7

UK Foreign Assets and Liabilities 1977Q4 - 2008Q2
(% of GDP)

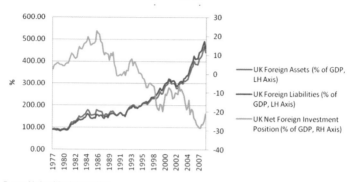

Source: National Statistical Office

Chart 8

UK Monetary Financial Institutions Assets, Foreign Currency Assets and Foreign Currency Liabilities 1998Q2 - 2008Q2
(% of GDP)

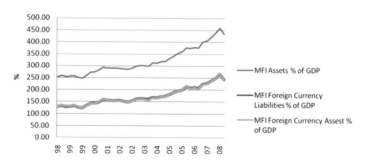

Source: National Statistical Office

But it is not just a matter of fiscal sustainability and the solvency of the state. The fact that sterling is not a global reserve currency, but the Euro is, will give Eurozone based financial institutions a competitive edge vis-à-vis UK based financial institutions. Global reserve currency status matters and can be a source of 'dark matter' (see Hausmann and Sturzenegger (2005)).

Other countries are (were) even more vulnerable than the UK to a run on the foreign currency deposits of their banks or to a locking up of foreign currency wholesale markets. Iceland (where gross financial assets and liabilities reached almost 800 percent of annual GDP at their peak in early 2007 and banking sector assets were around 900 percent of annual GDP) is an example. Switzerland is another one (banking sector assets are about 660% of annual GDP), aggravated by the fact that Switzerland is a Confederation where the central fiscal authority has very limited revenue raising powers. Unless a strong and solvent fiscal authority backs up the central bank, the central bank cannot hope to access a significant amount of foreign currency liquidity when an emergency strikes.

The UK is more like Iceland than like the US or the Eurozone when we consider the relative size of its financial sector and especially the size of its external balance sheet (see Charts 7 and 8). With gross foreign assets and gross foreign liabilities both close to 450 per cent of annual GDP, and with much of these assets and liabilities denominated in foreign currency, the UK is a highly leveraged entity - a hedge fund - and therefore vulnerable. In contrast, gross external liabilities of the US are around 100 per cent of GDP. And the US dollar is one of two serious global reserve currencies. Sterling, with 4.7 per cent of the stock of global reserves is a minor-league legacy reserve currency.

It is true that London has prospered with sterling in the past, even after sterling lost its world reserve currency status. But that was then - *then* being before the current global financial crisis. No-one had even considered the possibility that all systemically important financial wholesale markets would seize up at the same time, making lender-of-last-resort- and market-maker-of-last-resort support from the central bank essential for the very survival of the internationally active banks and a whole range of highly leveraged financial institutions.

The Bank of England can, at best, be an effective lender of last resort and market maker of last resort in foreign currency *at a cost* - a cost that will undermine the competitive advantage of the City. At worst, if the fiscal credibility of the UK authorities were to be in doubt also (not an inconceivable event, given years of procyclical budgetary policy), the Bank of England would not be able to operate at all as a foreign currency lender of last resort and market maker of last resort. A triple crisis – banking crisis, sterling crisis and sovereign debt crisis – could result.

There are just three ways to handle this problem. The first is to run down the international financial activities of the City even further than would be required in any case, even if the UK were to join the Eurozone, to undo the excessive financialisation of the UK economy. The second is to become the 51st state of the USA. The third is to adopt the Euro. Only the third one is feasible and reasonable.

Conclusion

Immediate UK membership in the Eurozone is dictated both by the conventional optimal currency area criteria (convergence, flexibility, labour mobility, fiscal flexibility) and by a new financial stability criterion: without Eurozone membership, the UK is more vulnerable to a triple financial crisis – a banking, currency and sovereign debt crisis - because it belongs to a group of countries characterised by the inconsistent quartet: (1) a small country with (2) a large internationally exposed banking sector, (3) a currency that is not a global reserve currency and (4) limited fiscal capacity relative to the possible size of the banking sector solvency gap.

Eurozone membership would eliminate the third member of the quartet. By reducing liquidity risk premia, it may even provide some minor relief as regards the fourth member of the quartet.

The case for waiting any longer with a UK application for Eurozone membership has been fatally undermined by the financial crisis that threatens to inflict lasting damage on the UK economy. The time to join is now.

Willem Buiter - Former member of the Bank of England Monetary Policy Committee. Professor of European Political Economy; European Institute, London School of Economics and Political Science; CEPR and NBER.

Sovereignty, Democracy and the Euro

The Queen's head on the pound note is a symbol of British sovereignty. By giving up the pound, would Britain lose its sovereignty? Does it matter? In this paper I will discuss two concepts of sovereignty and how they are related to modern democracy. I will argue that a single currency requires a European democracy as the next step in European integration. By joining the Euro, Britain could make a great contribution for a more democratic Europe.

Stefan Collignon

Two concepts of sovereignty

The meaning of sovereignty is extremely controversial. Two concepts dominate the debate. The traditional, pre-democratic notion defines sovereignty as a property of the King's authority that allows him to be the ultimate law-maker of last resort. The King had the ultimate authority to appoint agents of power - ministers and governments and courts - who would make and execute laws, hopefully in the public interest.[1] The source of this authority was derived from divine will and could not be questioned by men. Individuals were "subjects", not "citizens"; society was structured hierarchically. The English Revolution broke with this concept. Parliament challenged the King's authority. The House of Commons was to "represent" ordinary people, although the modern democratic principle of representation by universal and equal adult franchise became only fully accepted after the Second World War.

The modern conception of sovereignty was formulated with utmost clarity by the American and French revolutions. "We, the people" became the sovereign. Not divine will, but the Social Contract between all individual citizens was the source of modern sovereignty. As partners to this Social Contract, citizens were bound together by rights and obligations and they could appoint a government as the agent to execute their common will. "Representation" was no longer the symbolic presence of the nation in the person of the King, but the title of attorney to act on behalf of the owners of public goods.

This modern concept of sovereignty was grounded in the economics of markets and the monetary economy. Commercial transactions were often made "on behalf" of groups of investors. The development of banks and financial contracts propagated the idea that free and equal individuals could negotiate the terms of their commitments. The emergence of the monetary market economy therefore laid the ground for replacing traditional values of hierarchy by a new vision of individual freedom. At the same time it transformed the concept of the nation: the enlarged tribal family with the King as the patriarchal authority became a society where individuals had trust for each other and felt their national identity. This change reflected

[1] The eternal debate about corrupt governments is precisely caused by the perception that political agents serve themselves rather than the common good.

the new economic culture of financial contracts which were based on trust ("My word is my bond" was the motto of the Stock Exchange). We are more likely to trust people who are "like us" and distrust the foreign. The Queen on the pound note symbolizes both – the relation of trust among her subjects and of national identity.

Sovereignty and the idea of democracy

But trust is not enough. It needs to be backed up by law. The modern nation state became the synthesis of trust and law. It required a coherent form of government. Not by coincidence did the world's largest customs union with its common market and single currency unify its system of government in the early 18th century: The Articles of Union, which enacted the United Kingdom in 1707, stated in paragraph 3 "that the United Kingdom of Great Britain be presented by one and the same Parliament, to be styled the Parliament of Great Britain."[2] Can Europe with its common market and a single currency avoid a similar destiny?

The Union of England and Scotland in 1707 was still far from a democracy. Efficiency may have called for one government; but such an institution also needed legitimacy. Ideas of democracy had barely started to emerge. John Locke had been dead for only 3 years. The transition from the traditional to the modern concept of political sovereignty was a painful process and the controversy still inspires the debate about Europe. No country has made a greater contribution to this transition than Britain. She has shaped the most fundamental ideas in modern political philosophy and put them into historic reality. The repressiveness of the old hierarchical concept of sovereignty during the Restoration period led John Locke in the late 17th century to challenge the Tories and formulate the founding principles of liberal democracy. Without these ideas, the American Revolution would have been unthinkable and without Jefferson the *Déclaration des Droits de l'Homme et du Citoyen* of 1789 could not have set the tone for the next 200 years of struggle for democracy.

Today, we take democracy for granted. The fall of the Wall in Berlin, the disappearance of the communist empire, the emergence of a

2   Neil MacCormick, 1999. *Questioning Sovereignty. Law, State and Practical Reason.* Oxford University Press

Stefan Collignon

global market economy have established the principles of modern democratic governance as the undisputed foundations for a modern society. While some countries, most prominently China, fight rear guard battles, the direction of history is clear. But the struggle for democracy is never over. September 11th stands for the challenge of modernity by traditional fundamentalism. And even in Europe all is not well. Populists distort democracy in the name of democracy and Eurosceptic Tories all over Europe seek the return to narrow nationalism. The European Union is in a profound, structural crisis. At its root is the growing democratic deficit.

European democracy?

The rejection of the Lisbon Treaty by referendum in Ireland, following similar defeats of the Constitutional Treaty in France and the Netherlands carry a clear message: European citizens want a different Europe. Dissatisfaction is growing about the lack of democracy in Europe. Even profoundly pro-European citizens have voted against Europe, because they fear that the EU is heading in a direction they do not understand, approve, or control. What European citizens want is a more democratic Europe.

Politicians and intellectuals often explain the democratic deficit by the distance between European institutions and ordinary citizens. Multinational bodies, they claim, lack the grounding in common history, culture, symbolism and trust, on which most national polities draw. They recommend decentralization and subsidiarity as remedies. If their arguments were right, we should expect massive voter turnout in local elections and less at national elections. The opposite is the case. This analysis of political disenchantment misses the essential point of modern sovereignty, which is that citizens have the right to choose and appoint a government to manage their common public goods.

The democratic deficit reflects the fact that citizens are losing the sense of being the ultimate authority for political decisions. Technocratic decisions and *la pensée unique*, which Margaret Thatcher called TINA (There Is No Alternative), seem to make it irrelevant what people vote for. And most importantly, in

Stefan Collignon

Europe more and more policy decisions have become subject to intergovernmental compromises at the European level, which cannot be undone or even amended by democratically elected parliaments at the national level. National democracy is hollowing out because policies are made "in Bruxelles", but there is no democracy at the European level. Hence, citizens are no longer the ultimate collective law-maker. Governmental bureaucracies are. Governments are claiming to be sovereign, at the expense of "their" citizens. It is as if citizens belonged to governments (as earlier they belonged to the king), instead of governments belonging to citizens.

Following a line of juridical thinking that goes back to anti-democratic thinkers like Carl Schmitt, the German Constitutional Court has argued in its decision on the Maastricht Treaty, that there can be no democracy in Europe because there is no European people, no *demos*. This line of thinking values the feeling of identity higher than the rational interests of citizens. It has brought nothing but trouble, war and disaster to European history. We cannot build a peaceful Europe on tribal feelings of identity.

The European Commonwealth

A modern and democratic approach to Europe defines competences for jurisdictional levels of policy-making by the externalities of public goods. It views citizens not as subjects of their community but as the ultimate owners of public goods. "We" own public goods that affect "us". Citizens do not "belong" to their community, but the community is defined by the group of citizens who are potentially affected by the public goods which belong to them. This is what English political thought has so beautifully described as the *Commonwealth* and what the French idea of the Republic, the *res publica*, has echoed.

European citizens are the owners of different public goods, some of which are local and affect them in their immediate vicinity, others at the level of their nation and some have shared consequences for all Europeans. For example, hospitals are local public goods, education is a national public good and the European economy is a public good owned by all those who live in the European Union.

67
Stefan Collignon

The introduction of the Euro as a common currency to all citizens has significantly increased the range of European public goods. All citizens in the Euro Area are affected by European-wide inflation, interest rates, and the exchange rate to the dollar. They are concerned by policy decisions that affect these economic variables.

As owners of public goods, citizens in democracies appoint governments as their agents to administer these goods in accordance with their preferences. Because they are affected by the consequences of policy decisions, they must have the right to choose between different policies and to revoke their agent if they so wish. But making collective decisions requires also structures and institutions that allow them to deliberate together on what policy decisions serve their interests bests. Hence, if different public goods affect citizens at different levels, they must also be able to appoint different governments to administer these goods at each level. They must deliberate together before electing their government and this requires politicizing policy-making at the European level.

National governments cannot administer European public goods efficiently, because they do not represent European citizens who are the collective owners of European public goods. National governments draw their legitimacy from a limited local constituency and they are chosen for issues that have little to do with Europe. The European Council, as the ultimate decision-making body in Europe cannot be revoked by all those European citizens, which are concerned by their decisions. If England once had a Long Parliament, the European Council is like a Permanent Parliament. Who would seriously claim a system to be democratic, that appoints its representatives only by by-elections without ever calling for a General Election?

A European government

For half a century, European integration has progressed at an extraordinary pace. It has created more and more public goods that have increased the wealth of citizens. Today, these public goods need to be managed, and they need to be managed well. This is a matter of interest, and not of feelings. It has nothing to do with national

Stefan Collignon

identities. Conservative mainstream politicians seek to re-legitimize European integration by strengthening policy coordination between member state governments in order to produce better results ("deliveries"). They do not understand that the voluntary policy coordination between 27 governments makes attaining good results, rather than compromises based on the smallest common denominator, increasingly difficult, while at the same time it contributes to the deepening of the democratic deficit.

A modern conception of sovereignty requires that citizens can appoint an agent, a European government, which takes care of their interests as European citizens. Just as the European Economic Community required monetary union as its complement, so does the Euro call for a European political union with fully democratic structures, where citizens are the sovereign, not governments. It calls for Europe of citizen *in* lieu of l'Europe *des nations*, which still dominates conservative thinking from Sarkozy to Cameron.

Traditional concepts of federalism do not provide a solution to Europe's crisis of legitimacy. Under the label of subsidiarity, federalists demand more decentralized decision-making, arguing that people "belong" to local and cultural communities, in which they find their identity. For these supporters of *"Europe as a Federation"*, the European crisis is due to an excessive centralization of policy making at the European level. They do not understand that 50 years of European integration has produced a high degree of interdependence between EU member states where policy decisions made by one government have external effects for citizens in most or all other member states.

Euro-nationalists, who sympathize with the European Federalist Movement founded by Altiero Spinelli in 1943, emphasize the need for creating a European sense of community and identity by focusing on what unites European citizens. Yet they have remained powerless because they do not transcend the communitarian perspective of belonging and identity; they only seek to replace one idea of community by a different one (European rather than national). But the annoying reality is that people continue to define themselves in national terms before they accept their European identity. European federalists lack a clear criterion for justifying why and which policy decisions should be delegated to the European level.

Thinking of the European Union with its single currency as a European Commonwealth enables us to overcome today's legitimacy crisis of the integration project: it allows a unified approach to producing results in the interest of all citizens. It puts citizens firmly in charge of defining these interests and controlling the government that acts on their behalf.

In concrete terms, the European Political Union (EPU) would have to be based on a new Constitutional Treaty, which supplements the existing Treaty of the European Union and delimits European public goods from national public goods. It must provide the instruments for efficient and democratic policy making in the EU.

As the former Belgian Prime minister Guy Verhofstadt has pointed out[3], the logic of public goods, which affect all citizens across Europe, would require a European government responsible for policy making in the following domains:
- Macroeconomic management of the Euro Area, including the European budget
- Large European projects for technological research and development
- A single European area of justice and security to fight crime more effectively
- European diplomacy
- A European intervention force

All other policy areas should remain under the competence of national governments because they do not cover all citizens jointly. Of course, in cases of significant partial externalities, national authorities and the European government must assume their joint responsibility for policy making (shared competences).

The EPU would need to have a democratically elected government. In concrete terms this implies:
- Upgrading the European Commission into a European executive

---

[3]   Guy Verhofstadt. 2006. *The United States of Europe*. The Federal Trust, London

Stefan Collignon

- Electing the President of the Commission by the European Parliament and not by the European Council
- Giving him the power to formulate the broad policy orientations and to appoint other Commissioners to policy portfolios that administer European public goods
- The European Council remains the organ through which member state governments express their legitimate interests. The European Council serves as the second chamber in the legislative process of the EPU.

Are these demands ambitious, even too ambitious, for Europe? Maybe. But they are derived from the norms and principles of modern democracy – and there is hardly a European citizen who would question these values. Trying to duck the issue will only reinforce the dissatisfaction with European integration and is contrary to citizens' interests.

Is it counterproductive to raise these issues in the UK today, when joining the Euro is just barely re-appearing on the agenda? I do not think so. Joining the Euro means joining a monetary economy where the nature of policy externalities will significantly increase. It will create new bonds of trust among citizens. Sharing the same currency, operating in a large single market is creating new interests shared by ordinary citizens. As Jean Monnet said: "We do not create coalitions between governments, we are uniting human beings." With the substantial increase of private contractual relations across borders in Europe, national identities become less important. The issue of the European social contract has now become unavoidable. More than any other country, Britain has shaped our modern understanding of the social contract, of freedom, equality and democracy. It would be a shame for all of us to miss the opportunity of building a democratic and modern Europe together.

Stefan Collignon - Former Director of the Association for the Monetary Union of Europe. Former Professor at the London School of Economics and Harvard University. Now Professor at S. Anna School of Advanced Studies, Pisa.

The European Consequences of David Cameron

The Conservative Party was once a party of power, pragmatic in its policy orientation, realistic in its political behaviour and pro-European in instinct.

Today it has abused those fine traditions. It is rigidly ideological in its EU policy, unrealistic even delusional in behaviour towards EU institutions and anti-European in its gut.

This sad state of affairs would be less tragic if the Party did not now enjoy a possibility of wielding power in the near future. Uniquely

73
Nick Crosby

amongst all the 27 Member States there is now the chance that a major opposition party will come into office whose effective EU stance is either withdrawal or - more brutally- to provoke a crisis of membership that will either force the UK to leave or cause the EU to fragment, possibly fatally. This is the potential crisis that dare not speak its name.

Consider: in the mid 1990s, a weaker and less anti-EU conservative government than the prospective one, nevertheless degenerated into open declarations of anti Europeanism, conducted a 'beef war' with EU institutions and adopted an 'empty chair' in the Council of Ministers. Over beef! (A legitimate health worry for our partners and not only in the EU- Canada and the US and most of the world banned it.) Senior ministers, such as John Redwood came close then to advocating withdrawal from the EU.

That was then. And what of a future Conservative government? The prospective government will be stronger than in the 1990s, united around a visceral anti-Europeanism. The Tory civil war over the EU is over: the antis have won. There are a few honourable pro-EU Tories who uphold the tradition but they are dwindling. A distinguished MEP of long service described himself as belonging to the 'Pro European wing of the Conservative Party—or rather, feather'. The wise heads and experienced Conservative Europeans are ageing- they are tolerated by the younger antis who believe that tomorrow belongs to them.

Look at the young thrusters in the Party and you see an almost universal anti-Europeanism. Amongst the MEPs- Dan Hannan, who is openly allied to the 'Better Off Out' campaign that wants the UK to leave the EU (patron Norman Tebbit). Or Douglas Carswell, MP for Harwich and Clacton, also allied to the Better Off Out campaign, who is touted as one of the Party's sparkiest thinkers, a former adviser to Cameron and described by the Sunday Times as 'One of the energetic young Tory modernisers elected to the Commons in 2005.' Nick Herbert, the shadow justice minister cut his political teeth on anti-European campaigns, (Business for Sterling). And so on. Previously maverick anti-Europeans such as John Redwood have been rehabilitated and are leading policy development. No leading Tory politician with a future ahead of him or her sits on any pro-EU organisation such as the European Movement. (Ironic since Churchill was one of its founders.) The Conservative Party is now ideologically anti-EU and this is deeply rooted.

What of the senior players, Shadow Foreign Secretary Hague and the Leader David Cameron?

Hague's anti-European beliefs are well known. When he was leader in the 2001 election he famously campaigned with the slogan '7 Days to save the pound.' He sees the EU as somehow old fashioned, stifling enterprise and undemocratic in its structures. But specific policy alternatives to the Lisbon Treaty or to the EU have not flowed from him. Hague is very vague. One has to infer a policy.

One place to start inferring a policy was his address in October at the last Conservative Party conference. The speech deserves scrutiny. Unhappily, the one specific pledge he made on Europe—at a time of major economic crisis, increased political tensions with Russia and a new American President taking office—a moment for statesmanship one would think and clear European strategy and solidarity—is to pick a fight with the EU and effectively 'March on Brussels' over the Lisbon Treaty: 'If in the end this treaty is ratified, by all 27 nations of the EU, then clearly it would lack democratic legitimacy here in Britain, political integration would have gone too far, and we would set out at that point the consequences of that and how we would intend to proceed.'

Having opened up the possibility of a major crisis and issued a threat, Hague then backed-off from indicating the substance of what that negotiation would be about. Hardly guaranteed to win friends in the world and influence them. Others have been more direct. Norman Tebbit, celebrating the tenth anniversary of Margaret Thatcher's Bruges speech suggested: "I hope that the Conservative Party will set out a negotiating brief that the next Conservative government will take to Brussels early in its next term and that it would within two years of the next election present to the British people the outcome of its negotiations.

"Then in a referendum the British people would decide whether to accept what was on offer or simply to leave the Union. We cannot drift on as we have been; it is not fair either to the British people or to the European Union.

"We need to show Thatcherite courage and determination to lead the country along that path."

A variant of this scenario has also been mooted by some Conservative advisers. The government would seek major derogations from key common policies, e.g. fisheries, CAP, social chapter, and possibly competition policy. This would then be endorsed in a referendum and then presented to the other partner governments as a basis for renegotiation (read crisis.) The thinking is that the UK has in the past successfully bargained for a special deal, principally over CAP rebates under Thatcher. This would be an ambitious, larger version of that. Moreover, the UK would hold back from any deeper cooperation in foreign affairs and EDSP, on the premise that without a fully engaged UK the Union is emasculated- a massive form of 'non-cooperation.'

Of course, such major derogations are not nearly comparable to budget payments/adjustments. They strike at the core of the idea of the EU- supranational and common institutions, rule of law, common policies, the idea of political unity. Perhaps the best the Tories could achieve would be EEA-style status- a half member lacking any meaningful input to the EU's policy formation or leadership, yet bound by most of the Single Market legislation. The most likely outcome is that the blackmail is seen down by other EU governments, there is an almighty crisis (compounding the already exposed state of the UK's economy outside the Eurozone) and the choice falls between full commitment or exit.

Hague's speech is also important for what it didn't say and for the implied foreign policy philosophy behind it. The success of the EU at bringing peace, prosperity and security to the Continent was grudgingly conceded but there was no sense that the EU had a role in wider international affairs or that key states e.g. China and Russia see an integrated Europe as either a potential partner (the Chinese would like the EU to be more coordinated as it eases its economic relationships, one telephone number etc..) or a threat (the Russians fear EU solidarity as it offsets their potential political revival in their near abroad and counters their temporary dominance in Western energy supply. Hague's speech was highly intergovernmental and bilateral in its approach- as if the British foreign secretary alone or occasionally with the Americans could solve Afghanistan, climate change, stamp out terrorism in Pakistan etc...

There was no sense that the EU was anything more than a committee of nation-states, much like the UN- no hint that we shared common institutions and that we collectively were already acting on the world stage (conducting over 20 European missions from Africa to the Balkans). There was no sense that only via the EU could the UK deploy any credible international influence over major issues such as energy security, climate change, immigration and terrorism.

Hague's language was also revealing about how he sees the relationship between EU member-states and our common institutions. Bluntly, he denied there were any EU institutions. Everything was couched in phrases such as 'European nations 'doing stuff when the reality is that European nations can only meaningfully act within the EU framework. For example on Iran: 'Unless Iran responds positively in the coming weeks to the latest proposals, we call for EU nations to adopt progressively tougher measures against Iran, including a denial of access to Europe's financial system and a ban on new investment in Iranian oil and gas fields.' Why didn't Hague call upon the EU to adopt such measures, for the commission or the council to act- as these are the only effective ways of bringing European power to bear? Similarly, in facing down Russia in Georgia, Hague's formulation was 'The best chance of avoiding such conflicts in the future is for western nations to show what we have advocated: the strength of united resolve'. United resolve- how? Surely via the EU-- through strengthening the EU foreign policy machine and beefing up the ESDP- precisely what the Lisbon Treaty proposed and Hague opposed.

Herein lies the delusion and contradiction at the heart of the Conservative approach to the EU. Hague is clear that the world is

77
Nick Crosby

unstable, there are powerful economic challengers such as India and China, terrorism and security issues rear their ugly heads- yet he denies the EU any meaningful part in solving them, instead encouraging individual states to do their own thing. Or if they must collaborate, he gives no sense of how this should be done outside the EU framework.

For example, in opposing Russian aggression on Georgia, Hague urged: '…it should not be difficult for all the nations of democratic Europe to say this to the people of Georgia: that your right to live in peace and freedom was long-awaited and hard-won, that your democracy has every right ultimately to join the alliances of the world's democracies, and that the bullying of you or your neighbours must never be allowed to pay.' Sure- individual nations of democratic Europe can issue fine statements- we did that in the 1930's- but how do we take common action? By what instruments and policies? In what fora do we meet? Where and how do we commit the resources to go beyond words to action that deters aggression? How do we ensure European solidarity and follow-through? These are the practical questions- conservative questions of pragmatism and experience that one would expect a conservative foreign secretary to answer. Hague can't answer, because the answer is: through the EU. Hague's ideological aversion to the EU prevents him from seeing sense and offering real solutions and hope to our European neighbours.

What of David Cameron?

The one concrete act of Mr Cameron on EU matters has been to pull his MEPs out of cooperation and association with EPP_ED members in the European Parliament—a massive snub to the parliament, a sop to extreme anti-Europeans and UKIP, a move that denies his MEPs access to key committee chairs, roles and influence. And a symbolic gesture that says: We do not share the political ambitions of our sister parties in the EU or the EU generally.

Initially, commentators thought that this move was purely tactical, a means to secure his leadership of the Party. However, Cameron has gone beyond pulling out his MEPs: he has set up an alternative right bloc around a think tank the Movement for European Reform (MER) whose objectives are a different EU from the one on offer: ' ..leaving the EPP, the European People's Party, Parliamentary Group in the European Parliament…The reason is simple - which is that while we agree about open markets and deregulation we don't share their views about the future development of Europe.' (July 2006) And the MER: "Fifty years ago, a generation joined together to lay the foundations for the European Union. It was their response to the urgent challenges they faced: a divided Continent; economies ruined by war.

Now it is our generation's turn to lead. We welcome this opportunity, and we want to create a Europe that people can be proud of. But the Europe we are inheriting has become too inward-looking and inflexible, and is losing peoples' trust. The EU needs to change if it is to be a force for good in the world in the 21st century."

The details of his new EU are still to be worked out. At the last MER conference it was significant that many of the speakers were either well known Eurosceptics or mavericks. There is no worked out alternative and many of the speakers have contradictory agenda. For example, one session was framed as 'Free and Fair Trade'- almost a contradiction in terms, inviting enemies of the EU from a hardline free-trade or managed trade/development agenda to mutually attack the EU.

Cameron's political philosophy is classic New Tory: burnished in the heat of Thatcherism, a devotee of small government, minimal state, libertarian, and a populist anti-European: he has little experience of the Continent and perceives common EU institutions and supra-nationalism as either centralising, undemocratic or inefficient-probably all three.

Quite how his philosophy, his actions and his instincts will play out over the EU remains a mystery. One infers a vision for the EU, which Cameron would describe as 'modern' which is in fact a return to failed UK policies of the 1950s/1960s- an inter-governmental EFTA-style body that critically lacked any political clout or ability to exercise power in the international arena.

Under Cameron, the Conservatives would oppose Britain joining the Euro, would oppose strengthening of the EU's foreign policy machine and would seek a major political confrontation over the Lisbon Treaty reforms. This at a time of heightened economic crisis; at a time when his own shadow foreign secretary said the foreign policy 'challenges may be the most serious for any incoming government since the end of the Second World War'; and major competitors and neighbours such as Russia are actively dividing and ruling us Europeans.

The European Consequences of David Cameron could be devastating to the citizens of Europe, to the safety and economic prospects of the British people and to the idea of international democracy and the EU's founding principles. I urge all Conservatives to reclaim your tradition, reclaim your senses and reclaim your strong sense of the practical common solutions we Europeans deserve. Adopting the Euro would be such a positive step.

Nick Crosby - Director of the European ideas and discussion network, the Jean Monnet Circle. Formerly financial services consultant for PwC and now an internet entrepreneur.

The Silence of the Lambs

In response to the gathering global financial and economic crisis, occasional voices, notably that of Frank Field MP, have been raised in the United Kingdom, canvassing the possibility of a national government embracing all the main political parties. Whatever the general likelihood of such an arrangement, there is an important area of economic policy where a de facto national government already exists in this country, namely the European single currency. The Labour government, the Conservative Opposition and the Liberal Democrats are united in their view that the topic is one resolutely to be ignored, with at best occasional passing references to the impossibility of joining the Euro in any foreseeable future. It might be tempting to believe that this unusual unanimity reflects the

Brendan Donnelly

considered, measured and rational view of the British body politic on the question of the Euro. In fact, it is much more plausibly to be regarded as yet another proof of the dysfunctionalism of the British political system where European questions are concerned.

Few historians doubt that over the ten years of his Chancellorship, Mr. Brown acted as a substantial barrier to the well-documented desire of Mr. Blair to hold and win a referendum to secure British membership of the Euro. Quite apart from any considerations of personal rivalry towards the Prime Minister which may have weighed with Mr. Brown, his barely concealed hostility towards the Euro was based upon his well-publicised analysis of the supposed distinctness of the United Kingdom from and its superiority to the outdated and unreformed economies of its neighbours in Western Europe. Unlike France and Germany, the United Kingdom had understood the need in the modern world for radical economic and particularly financial liberalisation, which found its appropriate expression in high levels of personal and corporate debt in the United Kingdom, an ever-growing financial sector and an ever-rising property market which was indispensable to sustain British economic activity in general and personal consumption in particular. The successful distinctness of the British model would be put at risk by too close an association through the Euro with the European economic laggards who had not understood the way in which economic history was tending.

It is difficult to overstate the extent to which recent events have disproved the apparently plausible analysis on which Mr. Brown has relied over the past decade to justify his dismissive attitude towards the Euro. In so far as Britain did have in recent years an economic model distinct to itself, those distinctive characteristics are now shown to have been dangerous errors, ensuring that the recession on which most of the developed world is now entering will be more severe in the United Kingdom than for any of its neighbours. It is difficult to believe that the British financial sector will ever again be the provider of jobs, income and tax revenue that it has been in recent years. The now declining British property market will act as a multiplier of economic downturn in recession, as it acted as an economic multiplier in happier times. The dizzying decline in the external value of the pound may well lead in due course to difficulties in financing British governmental debt, which even on governmental assumptions generally regarded by commentators as over-optimistic, is likely to reach 8% of British GDP in 2009.

In these circumstances, it might have been expected that Mr. Brown would have demonstrated some willingness at least to reconsider that option of policy, his refusal to join the Euro, which was the most direct consequence of his flawed analysis of the relative merits of the somewhat (but only somewhat) differing economic structures on opposite sides of the English Channel. No such reconsideration seems remotely in prospect. It is difficult to avoid the impression that this refusal has at least as much to do with a desire to avoid an implicit admission that mistakes were made in the past as with a dispassionate evaluation of changed circumstances. It would be embarrassing to Mr. Brown implicitly to admit by reconsidering the question of British membership in the Euro that his well-publicised triumphalism about the supposed success of the British economy under his stewardship was greatly overstated. The current political culture of the United Kingdom, particularly as exemplified by the predatory mass media, suggests that no such admission will be forthcoming, at least until the publication of Mr. Brown's eventual memoirs, if then.

In another political culture than that of the United Kingdom, the Opposition might well now pressing for rapid movement by the government to join the Euro. Mr. Brown's political opponents would understand that to force him to reconsider the question of British membership of the European single currency would be a peculiarly potent recognition of political and economic defeat from New Labour. But if Mr. Brown is unlikely to accept any such reconsideration on his own initiative, he is even less likely to come under pressure to do so from the Opposition. Mr. Cameron's Conservatives are constrained from brandishing this powerful weapon with which to assault the government, not merely by their own visceral Euroscepticism but by the political choices and the rhetoric they employed throughout the whole course of Mr. Brown's Chancellorship.

It cannot be over-stressed that between 1997 and Mr. Cameron's accession to power in 2005, Euroscepticism was the undisputed motivating force of all the Conservative Party's political action. Mr. Cameron is no enthusiast for the European Union, but does understand that the electorate are easily bored or alarmed by obsessional concentration on the European issue from their leaders. Under his predecessors, however, the vainglorious claims of Mr. Brown that the British economy was demonstrably outstripping its European neighbours received nothing like the critical scrutiny that they deserved. The idea that continental European economic structures were demonstrably inferior to those of the United Kingdom, sedulously promoted by Mr. Brown, was one deeply congenial to the Eurosceptic Conservative Party. That this idea reinforced Mr. Brown's unwillingness seriously to contemplate British membership of the Euro could only render this fundamentally flawed analysis yet more attractive to the Conservative Party.

As a result of this equivocal approach in recent years by the Conservative Party to the questionable account given of his economic policies by Mr. Brown, Mr. Cameron and his colleagues have found themselves severely constrained in the critique they can now offer of Mr. Brown's economic record. For the past decade, they have always implicitly and frequently explicitly supported precisely those elements of the Prime Minister's general economic approach which are now shown to have been fundamentally flawed. There were not many Conservative spokesmen in recent years arguing that the oft-praised American economic model was one bringing with itself considerable risk for a medium-sized economy such as that of the United Kingdom. This long-standing objective complicity in the economic policies of New Labour has ensured that the criticism offered of Mr. Brown's current economic policies by the Conservatives has been partial and opportunistic, and the electoral advantage derived from it uncertain and patchy. Mr. Cameron's recent attempts to draw a clear line between himself and Mr. Brown on the question of new debt are a clear attempt to distract attention from the fact that his party has been at least as much in prey as Mr. Brown since 1997 to the myth of a robust, successful British economy striding purposefully ahead of its sluggish continental competitors. The explicit rejection of this myth would lead Mr.

Cameron and his Eurosceptic Party along what would be for them dangerous paths, which they are understandably unwilling to explore too thoroughly.

The "Westminster consensus" on the subject of the Euro has recently obtained a new recruit in the form of the Liberal Democrats, traditionally the most pro-European party of the British political spectrum. The document on party policy adopted at their party conference in September 2008 could say no more than that "there may before long be a case for a renewed hard-headed debate" on the issue. As the representation of the Liberal Democrats has grown in Westminster, their MP's have sought increasingly to adapt themselves to the insular preoccupations and prejudices of the House of Commons. Liberal Democrat MPs have in consequence become more and more reluctant to differentiate themselves from the British Parliamentary mainstream by unseemly displays of enthusiasm for the European Union. This process of "socialisation" into the culture of the House of Commons has been reinforced by the fact that a substantial proportion of Liberal Democrats come from the supposedly Eurosceptic South West of England. Many of these MPs believe that their chances of re-election will be improved if they are seen to distance themselves from the public enthusiasm for the European Union that until recently was the orthodoxy of their party. The sea change which has taken place in the attitudes of Liberal Democrat Members of Parliament to European questions was well illustrated by their failure to agree a common position on the Lisbon Treaty when it passed through the House of Commons in February, 2008. A substantial proportion of the Liberal Democrat MPs were willing and eager to join with the Conservative Party in calling for a referendum on the Treaty, at a time when their leader, Nick Clegg, was vigorously arguing that the Lisbon Treaty was not a document apt for such plebiscitary consultation. There can be little immediate hope that the Liberal Democrat Party will be an effective standard-bearer for renewed consideration of the possible advantages accruing to the United Kingdom from early membership of the Euro.

Ironically, the Liberal Democrat MPs have sought to mute their public espousal of the Euro precisely at a time when British public opinion is becoming notably more open-minded about the merits of the single European currency. Even before the recent decline of sterling against the Euro, it had become obvious to any fair-minded British observer that the Euro was a well-established feature of the world's economic order, bidding fair in due course to rival the dollar as an international currency. The travails of the British financial sector and of its housing market were further factors reducing confidence in the British government's rosy predictions of an undisturbed path to a specifically British prosperity on the edge of the Eurozone. Commentators, letter-writers and academics calling for British membership of the Eurozone are today notably more numerous, albeit still in a definite minority, than they were even a year ago. It might be thought surprising that this unmistakable evolution of British public opinion currently finds no reflection whatsoever at the parliamentary level. The political history of the past decade does much to explain this apparent anomaly. There are many senior figures in all three major parties who believe that the United Kingdom will and should join the Euro. Through a mixture of complacency, wishful thinking and opportunism, they have spent the past ten years elaborating ever new excuses why "now" was not the time publicly to articulate these views.

The fecklessness of the pro-Europeans in the Conservative Party of the late 1990s found in the new century its sorry counterpart on European issues in the slippery evasiveness of the New Labour government of Mr. Blair. At a time when an obvious opportunity now presents itself to initiate and shape public debate on the Euro, prevarication on European issues has become for many potential leaders of a pro-Euro and pro-European discourse in this country such an ingrained a habit of mind that many are incapable of recognising, let alone seizing this opportunity. As often in the recent past, those incorrigibly hostile in this country to the European Union have judged the tactical situation much better than the Union's supposed advocates. There are clear signs from the recent utterances of leading Eurosceptic politicians and their allies in the City and the media that they see the potential harm done to their traditional stances on the Euro by recent events and are looking to browbeat the government away from political engagement on this, for them, dangerous ground. Grotesquely, political utterances from British

Brendan Donnelly

politicians against or studiedly neutral on the subject of the Euro have in recent times been infinitely more frequent than those well disposed towards or even willing positively to recommend British membership of the single currency.

These last ten years of silence or evasion on the Euro from those whose inner convictions were at variance with their public stances did much more to undermine rational debate on European issues in the United Kingdom than even the previous decade of Mrs. Thatcher's growing hostility to all things European and John Major's ineffectual manoeuvrings to hold together an imploding Conservative Party. The events of this period should be a warning and lesson of dangers arising from an excess of self-censorship and reluctance to stake out clear positions on European issues. If the leading figures of British politics who understand the need and desirability of full-hearted British involvement in the European Union repeat their mistakes of the recent past, the inevitable consequence of their further dilatoriness will be at least to postpone and perhaps to destroy for ever any chance of the United Kingdom's eventually becoming a member of the European single currency. There are powerful and well-organised forces within the United Kingdom utterly determined to frustrate British membership of the Euro. The path towards that membership, if finally undertaken, will in any event be a long and difficult one. There is no reason to believe that it will become easier or less demanding through further postponement of the time when this issue is fairly joined, with proponents of British membership of the Euro showing the same energy and commitment which the Euro's opponents, to their credit, have manifested over the past decade.

Tragically, the possibility of a British economic catastrophe in the short or medium term can no longer be dismissed out of hand. It is still unclear how severe a bill will be presented for a decade of economic incontinence. In the calamitous circumstances of manifest economic disaster, it is difficult to believe that British membership of the Euro could be other than an inevitable consequence of this new situation. But it is a strange conception of responsible political action simply to await potential disaster before drawing the lessons which disaster can teach. Most of those favourable to British membership of the Euro believe for their part that this threatening economic disaster could be mitigated, perhaps even warded off, by Britain's joining the Euro, or at least setting out a credible timetable for doing so. It will be a devastating commentary on the lack of political leadership shown on this matter by the British political elite over the past twenty years if their continuing hesitation and self-interested reticence serve merely to ensure that the United Kingdom can only join the Euro when this economic disaster is an accomplished fact.

Brendan Donnelly - Formerly at the Foreign and Commonwealth Office, the European Parliament and the European Commission. Member of the European Parliament (1994 to 1999) and a founder of the Pro-Euro Conservative Party (1999-2004.)

The Euro and Russia

In the eighteenth century, Russian policy towards Western Europe was largely determined by the extent to which divisions between the various fractious and disunited German states could be exploited. War with Napoleon, however, soon convinced statesmen in Saint Petersburg that a united Germany, under the leadership of Prussia, which had resolutely resisted the French Emperor, might offer a bulwark against French ambition and a useful partner with whom the peace of Europe might be guaranteed in the future. Bismarck developed close ties with Saint Petersburg and finally managed to persuade Russia to accept German unification in 1870.

Harold Elletson

The attitude of modern Russia to closer European integration has, until recently, been similarly ambiguous. The Kremlin has sought to exploit divisions between European states for its own political purposes, primarily in order to dilute perceived United States influence and to weaken the position of the various troublesome former captive nations of the Soviet Union. Bizarrely, in pursuit of this agenda, it has recently often found itself closely linked with right-wing, eurosceptic groups, such as Britain's Conservative Party (Vladimir Putin's United Russia Party, for example, even persuaded dim-witted Conservatives on the Council of Europe to enter into a formal alliance).

Whenever Russia has tried to undermine or limit the independence of the states on its periphery and the other former captive nations of Eastern Europe, it is to the European Union that they have turned for support. Just as the reunification of eastern and Western Europe was inspired in part by the ideal of European unity, so the new-found freedoms of Eastern Europe have been both guaranteed and nurtured by the European Union. To the citizens of Poland, the Baltic States or Romania, the prospect of ever-closer political and economic union with the rest of Europe has not been the stuff of the nightmare fantasies of British eurosceptics but their best hope of continued freedom, independence and economic development. To them, the ludicrous hysteria of Britain's anti-European ideologues and their absurd attempts to draw comparisons between "Brussels" and the Soviet Union must sound not only childish but irresponsible and even sinister.

Furthermore, Russian policy towards Europe is changing. The Kremlin has got the message. Europe's determination to press ahead with both 'widening' and 'deepening' has forced Moscow to rethink its old strategy of 'divide and rule.' Just as nineteenth century Russia eventually found that it could easily and advantageously come to terms with Bismarck's united Germany, so today's Russia is coming to terms with the idea of a new *'Ausgleich'* with the European Union.

Harold Elletson

The Russian Foreign Minister, Sergei Lavrov, told businessmen at the beginning of December that "the EU is Russia's closest neighbour and partner both in politics and the economy." He said that EU-Russian relations were "acquiring a new quality and we have every reason to describe them today as a strategic partnership."

There are several reasons for Moscow's change of tack. Two of the most important, however, are the success of the single European currency in the "Euro zone" and an acknowledgement of the importance of European markets as both a source of investment in, and consumption of, Russian energy. Russia has made a major switch in its policy of almost exclusively denominating its foreign currency reserves in US dollars to holding increasing amounts of Euros. As Russia is already the world's second biggest oil and gas producer, with enormous untapped potential in its vast undeveloped and unexplored hinterland, and with the likelihood that western European consumers will continue to look east to Russia as a source of affordable energy, the effect can only be to deepen the Russo-European partnership and make the Euro stronger.

Russia has realised that it needs a stable relationship with an economically strong and successful European Union. On its eastern border, as the population of Siberia falls into dramatic decline, it views the steadily growing prosperity and rising confidence of China with some unease. The western European market for Siberian energy, therefore, assumes a political, rather than merely an economic, significance for Moscow, as it creates a firm European interest in Russia's far-flung eastern provinces. As China slides smoothly into its new position as a global superpower, Russia will increasingly look to its relationship with the European Union to maintain its position.

Despite the pressures on the Russian economy, created by the recent global credit crunch, and despite the political opprobrium that it attracted as a result of its military intervention in Georgia during the summer, Russia is now more determined than ever to develop a close economic partnership with the European Union. This is unlikely to be greatly affected either by concern over the continuing interest of the United States in the former Soviet space (for example, over

91
Harold Elletson

the stationing of missile defence systems in Poland), by irritation at the West's criticism of its policies in the Caucasus and elsewhere or by its own attempts to cajole certain former Soviet countries into closer economic union. The energy base of the Russian economy will dictate its continuing partnership with Western Europe.

What will all this mean for Britain? Europe needs Britain's weight and experience to help shape a realistic and workable partnership with Russia. Such a partnership could guarantee long-term stability and prosperity for the whole continent. This prize will depend not merely on European finance and Russian resources but also on a strong currency and the determination of Europeans to take hold of their own destiny. To ignore the opportunity that now presents itself would leave the British economy dangerously exposed and be a betrayal both of future generations and of our true national interest. Now is not the moment for Britain to shrink from the challenge of leadership. It is no time for weakness, vacillation or idle dreams of past glory. It is time for Britain to take the leading role in setting the course for Europe's future.

Harold Elletson - Former Member of Parliament (1992 to 1997). Specialist on Russian and Eastern European affairs. Now Chairman of the New Security Foundation.

Mired in History and Ego

Since 1688 British political history has been marked by continuity. Bagehot and Whig historians constructed a credible case for a slowly evolving British polity, within which worldly scions of the aristocracy allied with creative outsiders, e.g., Burke, Disraeli and Lloyd George, to make prudent adjustments to the parliamentary system and the constitutional monarchy which provided its foundation. This version of Britain Past remains the conventional wisdom on display in political and media discourse. It is jolly useful to have a past with a long tale when unexpected events turn up, such as the deployment of British troops in Afghanistan. Journalists and historians are evoking the doughty Victorian ancestors who patrolled the Northwest Frontier on horseback. Against the background of

Britain's high military profile in world peacekeeping, the celebration of Remembrance Day in 2008 was particularly moving. As always, we were commemorating the men and women who had sacrificed their lives for Queen and country in the 1914-18 war and subsequent conflicts. The arrangement of the Cenotaph ceremony so that currently serving service-people were shepherding the veterans of the Great War underlined this continuity.

The relationship between the people inhabiting the island of Britain and their mainland European cousins has also been characterised by continuity. But its quality and significance have recently been contested. Euro-sceptics have short, selective memories. They choose not to remember Macmillan's recognition that membership of the Common Market was a pre-requisite to maintaining Britain's economic and political position in the world. They also want to forget that trade union leaders, from Ernest Bevin to Sam Watson and George Brown believed that British social democracy depended on close relations with European nation-states. (As chairman of the Labour NEC International Committee, Watson was a confidant of Gaitskell and tried to persuade him to discard his redundant imperial reflexes.)

The myth of the British people's aversion to the Common Market is a recent invention, creatively woven by spin doctors and nurses in the wake of Thatcher's *volte face* towards Europe after 1985, when Geoffrey Howe persuaded her to sign the Single European Act, which committed all member states to closer integration. (Having led Britain to victory in the Falklands war, she became a victim of her own success. Like Napoleon, she suffered from an onset of triumphalism and lost a realistic sense of proportion.) Michael Foot and Neil Kinnock, the leaders of the Labour Party in the 1983 and 1987 general elections, both came from the party's left flank, and had been consistent anti-Europeans in the Bevanite mould. Not surprisingly, they failed to challenge Thatcher's born again Euro-scepticism.

In 1997 the young men and women who buried the entrails of old Labour indecently soon after John Smith had been laid to rest declared that a new era of British history had begun. A commitment to making Britain truly part of Europe had been at the core of John Smith's social democratic beliefs, and Blair embraced it without qualification as a New Labour goal. It had been Old Labour whose centre-right leader, Hugh Gaitskell, had declared that neither he nor the party should be bound by geography. The Great British Labour Party were citizens of the world, not parochial Europeans. Old Labour's left-wing remained implacably hostile, agreeing with the French and Italian communists that the Common Market was a capitalist club. (They had reacted in the same way towards the European Coal and Steel Community, perceiving it as a threat to the sovereign National Coal Board.)

The 1997 general election manifesto duly pledged that New Labour would make a new beginning towards the European Union. Parliament was adjourned soon after it assembled for the first time under Prime Minister Blair. During the long recess expectations were high, assisted by magnificent summer weather and a thirst for champagne to celebrate the unexpected New Labour landslide. Rumours were rife that the Queen's Speech would announce Britain's intention of joining the single European currency.

Given the manifesto commitment to make a fresh start in Europe, such speculation was not idle gossip. Blair's European orientation was common knowledge. If the Cabinet had agreed in June to begin preparations for Britain joining the Euro, they would have encountered little opposition when parliament re-assembled in November. The speedy reversal of the Major government's position would have been viewed as a fair cop, the kind of dazzling political opportunism which the public had come to expect from their Tony.

It is important to pursue this counter-factual narrative. Most media commentators and political 'scientists' have fallen victim to hindsightism about the Blair government's *volte face* towards the Euro. They maintain that it was inevitable that Blair should have bowed to the intense pressure exerted by his Chancellor of the Exchequer and the Treasury. Because the British public and Rupert Murdoch were so profoundly Euro-sceptic, Blair's retreat from his firm intention to take Britain into the European single currency was simply not practical British politics.

But another outcome was certainly possible in 1997. There was widespread apprehension throughout the EU about the impending disappearance of separate national currencies and the emergence of the Euro. It was, after all, a significant change, particularly for Britain where the pound sterling had remained inviolate and unaffected by the political upheavals of the nineteenth and twentieth centuries in which many other European currencies had perished and been reborn. And, of course, the fabric of British everyday life remains rooted in a culture which assumes that very little changes— except the weather, which generates endless conversation and observation.

The counter-factual narrative relies on the fact that a critical mass of 'ordinary' British people, particularly those who reached adulthood after 1972, were neither anti-European nor Euro-sceptic. Being part of Europe was second nature, a normal part of their British lives. In the 1990s, after the Single European Market had become part of *acquis communitaire*, more and more younger Europeans came to live and work on this side of *la Manche*. Our indigenous culture was becoming not merely a post-colonial *melange*, but a veritable cosmopolitan goulash. Attracted by warmer weather, lower population densities and good wine, Britons of all classes were buying second homes or selling up and emigrating outright to France, Portugal and Spain. Hindsightists conveniently forget that Margaret Thatcher's fall from power was precipitated by Geoffrey Howe's resignation as deputy Prime Minister in 1990 for European *raisons d'etat*. They also ignore the support that he received from key occupants of the Tory front and back benches.

The British prejudice against substantial change could have been overcome by a determined Prime Minister Blair and his cabinet. Roy Jenkins' successful piloting of the transition to decimal currency, which took place in February 1971 under the Heath government, is an apt case in point. As someone who experienced decimalisation, I can recall the grumbling, scepticism and even anger with which many people over thirty greeted the arrival of one hundred pence to the pound. The Treasury's nerve held against the tide of regret over the disappearance of bobs and tanners. It is difficult today to imagine why we felt sentimental about the old system. A similar

96
Nina Fishman

sequence of events characterised the transition to the Euro in those countries which adopted it. Scepticism and sentimentalism for francs and marks before E-day, followed by acceptance and adjustment after it.

Unfortunately for the British people, the immoveable obstacles to Blair's plan that Britain should join the Euro at its creation were Gordon Brown and the Treasury. Blair was not stymied by popular Euro-scepticism or even by Rupert Murdoch's visceral dislike of European 'corporatism'. He was deflected by a Chancellor of the Exchequer who was determined to rule his Treasury realm with a rod of iron unencumbered by any European constraints. Brown's orientation was exclusively across the Atlantic. As a close observer saliently remarked, Brown had come to know and cherish the Ivy League and Cape Cod United States, whilst remaining apparently oblivious and incurious about the America of fundamentalist Christianity, Texas and the Middle West.

Brown approached global politics from a Panglossian perspective, not dissimilar to Gaitskell's fantasy of world citizenry. His intellectual canon stretches from the north eastern American seaboard to Liverpool and the Firth of Clyde, and then skirts Europe to engage with Delhi and Hong Kong. He has seen no need to acquire fluency in another European language and remains apparently untouched by knowledge of Britain's intimate political and cultural kinship with Europe.

From the point of view of Blair's European commitment, it was ironic that the most Atlanticist member of Blair's government should go to the Treasury. Unlike the Foreign Office, the Treasury had made an uneasy transition to thinking European in the 1970s. In the decade after Macmillan decided to apply for British membership of the EEC, the FO mandarins did their homework. Through their diplomatic networks, they already possessed a reservoir of knowledge which they turned to good effect. After British entry in 1973, seconded civil servants discovered how well British interests could be served through co-operation and consensus-seeking in Brussels. For the Treasury, however, the most important imperative remained the defence of sterling. The pound was the foundation of the Treasury's claim to be the top department of state. There is no economic reason for keeping the pound. As Samuel Brittan wrote in 2003, he had 'never regarded the direct economic effects of Euro membership as terribly important one way or the other'.[1]

The importance of the Euro for the British people is monetary. We need a stable, reliable means of international exchange. The urgent dilemma facing us and Gordon Brown is that global economic players have ceased to regard the pound sterling as a serious currency. They are betting that it will go on losing value in relation to the Euro. If the United Kingdom was a large economy which did not import many raw materials or manufactured goods, the pound's decline wouldn't matter very much to 'ordinary people'. But we are a small offshore island with little manufacturing strength and no significant natural resources except coal. We need the anchor of the Euro to maintain our current living standards.

In 2009 paper money has no intrinsic value. It acquires value to the extent that it is accepted in exchange for goods and services. It is a means of payment and source of credit. If economy 'A' uses conch shells as its currency, then traders from economy 'B' must acquire conch shells before they can buy the goods which manufacturers in economy 'A' produce. In the aftermath of World War II, cigarettes and nylon stockings were the means of payment used by millions of people in central Europe. These commodities functioned as currency because they were accepted by most economic players and had a reasonably stable value.

Dan Corry, currently employed at the No. 10 Policy Unit, observed in 1995, 'The key question for the UK is … [whether] Britain can sensibly stay outside. Much of this concerns the economics and politics of being in the second division....The Portillo style economy with flexible, gyrating, exchange rates, deregulated labour and capital markets and little social welfare may well be a tenable model for Britain as offshore island to the EU core. It is yet to be shown how a social democratic Britain could thrive outside a core,

---

1   Samuel Brittan, 'The Dubious Political Case for the Euro', *New Economy*, June 2003, reprinted in S.Brittan, *Against the Flow, Reflections of an Individualist*, Atlantic Books, London, 2005, pp.193-4.

Nina Fishman

single currency area.'[2] The vicissitudes of the credit crunch and current world recession have confirmed Corry's fourteen year's old conclusion. Although he is probably keeping his own counsel, it is unlikely that he has changed his mind.

For over a decade Gordon Brown's and the Treasury's attachment to sterling has prevented Britain from joining the Euro. They have placed the symbolic value of the pound, as an independent currency before its role as an international means of exchange. They have valued their own status as 'independent' actors on the world stage as more important than British citizens' economic security. Faced with the choice of keeping sterling and accepting a continuously deteriorating standard of living and joining the Euro, who, apart from UKIP diehards, is likely to vote to preserve the pound? Gordon Brown should ask the British people whether they want to abandon the pound and begin the preparations for entry into the Euro. He should hold the referendum now and let the people decide.

Nina Fishman - Honorary Research Professor, History Department, Swansea University.

---

2   Dan Corry, 'Restating the Case for EMU:--Reflections from the Left', Working Paper, Institute for Public Policy Research, London, September 1995, p.34.

The Euro and European Supervision – Does the UK being "out" matter?

When the Maastricht treaty was initially being drawn up many assumed that it would not matter much if the EU single market and the Euro area were not the same. There was relatively little debate as to whether it would make much difference if the single market for financial services which was being launched in the early 90s also had a single currency or not, and the idea of organising financial supervision on a pan-European basis was a pretty theoretical notion. Aside for the political debate, the financial focus was on whether it could make sense for a geographic area of such economic and fiscal diversity as the EU to have a single interest rate, not on what it meant for the City or for supervision.

101
David Green

Nonetheless, once it became clear that the UK was **not** going to join the Euro area at its inception, there began to be concern as to whether being "out" would damage the City or whether this would give a boost to the ambitions of Paris, Frankfurt or Milan to take over as European financial centres. And could the ECB start to exercise direct influence over banking supervision, if not supervision more widely, since most of those central banks whose governors would become the members of the ECB's Governing Council were also responsible for banking supervision?

For a while these concerns appeared to have been unjustified. As it turned out, after some tussle, a separate banking supervision committee at EU-wide level was created separate from the ECB, the Committee of European Banking Supervisors, and was physically located in London. This was part of a more general movement to separate banking supervision from the central bank, as had been done in the UK, and to set up separate integrated supervisors, often based on the model of the UK's FSA. This happened in Germany and in a number of the smaller countries in the Euro area.

Furthermore, as markets evolved a clear preference for London as the dominant financial centre of Europe emerged, the UK held its own in the construction of the Financial Services Action Plan, and it appeared not to have mattered after all that the UK had not joined. Thus, when Gordon Brown applied his "five tests" to check whether the case for UK Euro area membership had changed, there was no strong evidence that it mattered that London was "out"; a large proportion of the UK banking system was by then accounted for by Euro area-based banks, most significant firms in London were counterparties of the ECB and, indeed, London had become the key financial centre for Euro-denominated business.

The crisis we are now undergoing fundamentally challenges the assumption that non-participation does not matter for supervision. The critical nature of the relationship between a central bank and the supervisor has become the focus of intense interest everywhere. The ECB has had to engage in extraordinarily wide liquidity support operations that have caused it to want to know far more than in the past about what is going on inside banks. More fundamental questions are being asked. Perhaps the splitting up of responsibilities between central bank and supervisor had gone too far? Perhaps closer connections could have caused supervisors to be more proactive earlier? Is it right that the ECB provides liquidity support to banks headquartered outside the Euro area as well as those within?

The crisis has also shown that much more coherence is needed across countries in macroeconomic management. Crisis support operations for banks are equally seen to need to be coherent on a Euro area-wide basis. Perhaps, some say, this means that supervision needs to be organised on a Euro area-wide basis too.

A consequence of the crisis has been that, for the first time since the Euro area was created, the "Eurogroup" of countries participating in the Euro has had to meet at head of government level to discuss real, pressing business. These meetings are likely to continue, with the extended period of calm during which the meetings of Eurogroup finance ministers took few decisions, likely to be seen as abnormal. Euro area governments will want to continue to be sure that what has happened in their banking systems and which has seen such large scale intervention by the ECB as well as injection of public funds will not reoccur.

Already minds are turning afresh to the clause in the Maastricht treaty which has yet to be activated, but which gives the ECB a formal role in banking supervisory policy. The ECB's Banking Supervision Committee, which has provided a discussion forum for central banks and supervisors from across the EU, has recalled that it can meet in Euro area composition only, if so justified. In any case, the central bank governors from the main Euro area countries are already either already responsible for banking supervision or have a major role in it and so can discuss it amongst themselves whenever they meet, as they do at the ECB.

It has been noted too that, while many Euro area headquartered banks have been active in London, few British-based banks are active on any scale in the Euro area which means that the authorities' interest tends to be focused outside the EU. By contrast, now that many Euro area banks have had to be rescued by their governments, those governments may take an increasing interest in just where they do their business, and they have not been slow to point out that some at least of the more exotic business that has contributed to the crisis has had its origin in London.

Of course, the activation of a formal role for the ECB in banking supervision requires unanimity across the EU for it to be introduced and regulation still remains to be set at an EU-wide level. Nevertheless, once a consensus on supervisory matters has been forged within the Euro area, it could become quite difficult to resist, especially where a particular Anglo-American approach has become discredited.

It would perhaps be difficult to argue that it would be fatal for the UK not to be involved in such discussions, which will certainly take place, but the UK's position as a non-participant in the Euro means that the concerns of a decade ago that the UK might not be able to put its case in discussions of vital interest to its financial system have finally become justified.

David Green - Former Head of International Policy at the FSA.

Why Farmers Should Always Love the Euro

The most striking aspect about agriculture is that it is subject to so many variables which affect its profitability. The weather, in a foul mood, can wipe out a crop, especially in tropical regions. But when it is benign it can produce unmarketable surpluses. Although the consumption of food is stable, relatively small changes in demand can have a huge effect on prices – a 1% increase in demand can result in a price increase of 20% and more. Input costs, especially artificial fertilisers, can swing dramatically depending on oil prices. The fertility of land varies enormously across the world which means that those working poor quality soil, with consequent low

105
Chris Haskins

yields, can make a living when prices are good and costs low, it is not worth their while growing a crop when the reverse is the case.

Volatility arising out of soil and climate variations takes place at local and international levels. Food consumption trends are more global, with the prospering Asian demand for meat and dairy products rising steadily, thereby strengthening world prices. But the current economic turmoil will undoubtedly impact on food markets, with people eating less meat fruit and vegetables and more wheat, flour and rice.

Through the ages governments have been struggling to stabilise the situation by intervening in the markets to secure food supplies for their citizens, and at affordable prices. The EU's Common Agricultural Policy was a legacy of post-war food shortages, intended to make enough food available for everyone by using taxpayer's money to subsidise and incentivise the farmers to grow more. But so successful was the policy that it has been reversed in recent years, whereby farmers were required to grow less, because of the endemic surpluses which were arising. Now, with rising global demand, this policy has been largely abandoned. Instead farmers are given a "social" payment, which is not related to markets at all, but this "social" payment is given to large, prosperous landowners, and small, struggling ones alike.

Farmers' incomes therefore are extraordinarily volatile and unpredictable thanks to a combination of weather, market demand, oil prices and government intervention. But there is another crucial element – currency exchange movements. The dollar remains the main currency used in global food markets, and it has been extraordinarily volatile in recent years, particularly against the second most relevant currency – the Euro. Shortly after its launch the Euro was worth much less than a dollar. Now it stands at a dollar and a half.

British farmers have an additional factor affecting their incomes, which is the so-called independent British currency. Britain is a substantial net importer of food, and the vast majority of it comes from other parts of the EU – tariff free but exposed to the vagaries of the Euro/sterling exchange rate. Over the past 8 years the pound Euro rate has varied from 1-20 to 1-60 and back to 1-10. In the past 18 months alone the pound has fallen by nearly 30% against the Euro, creating an unexpected bonanza for British farmers, but in the admittedly unlikely event of sterling going back to its previous levels against the Euro, then they would be hard hit.

British food shoppers have suffered, as farmers have benefited, from the decline in the pound against the Euro. It would therefore benefit farmers and shoppers alike, if Britain was part of the Single Currency, because prices would be less volatile, and there is quite enough unpredictability in the world without having this unnecessary element.

This is a propitious time to extol the economic virtues of Britain joining the Euro. The present rate of exchange is realistic and farmers would, I believe, find it acceptable. The somewhat controversial five economic tests would surely be passed if they were applied. But the political likelihood of progress is non existent – a sceptical Prime Minister (who is still uncomfortable in the European Community), an implacably hostile conservative party, and a frightened liberal leadership. It remains the case that just as only a right wing American President could break the ice with China, so a chastened right wing British government could be forced to lead Britain into the Euro.

Chris Haskins - Former Chairman of Northern Foods. Now Chairman of the Open University and a farmer.

Securing Sustainable Capital Markets

In the early 1990s when I ran IPMA, the multi-currency primary Euro-capital market's trade body, bond underwriters were or at least saw themselves as the *zeitgeist*.

In truth this reflected the flavour of 1920s Wall Street. As the 1990s unfolded, sanctimonious references, again rehearsed in 2008, were made to remuneration practices valuing short term individual gain over institutional and market stability but the deed did not follow the word.

By the mid 1990s, the trends leading to 2008's financial meltdown were visible to anyone who cared to look: it is a matter of record that, for example, I spotted Barings' vulnerability before it crashed, a classic case of death following a short term feeding frenzy in the Far East.

In common with public debate about the UK's ideal monetary policy, financial services regulation failed to move with the times: as well as having been proved in 2008 beyond doubt to be unfit for purpose, this regulation has even been conceptually overtaken by the best of environmental regulation, something that would have seemed inconceivable at the end of the last century.

A well functioning and appropriately contextualised international market has a great capacity to make life better. It can encourage productive uses of capital to enhance prosperity and can enable corporate and governmental borrowers to raise funds on a basis enabling them to do more with less. Modern technologies give Europe a historically unprecedented opportunity to build an exceptionally strong and effective capital market.

Not all will agree with me that one necessary ingredient is ethical purpose. However, a sense of moral purpose persuaded European Member States, during the first harmonisation of financial services laws in the 1990s, to contemplate – in the context of longer term anticipation of a shared currency - a legal regime that in practice allowed sovereignty to be shared over what had been national savings pools.

Sadly, amorality within the market itself both shaped its evolution and undermined civic society.

It was not necessarily sinister that a European market developed as a result of US tax policies in the early 1960s. However, a core component of the Eurobond market's subsequent development was literally criminal as it was brazenly based on illegal tax evasion rather than lawful tax avoidance.

The notorious "Belgian dentist" travelling to Luxembourg to cash in interest on Eurobonds, without declaring or paying tax, was in every possible sense a saboteur of the wider European project.

He exacerbated a gap between the word and deed of Belgian law. He contributed to Belgium's subsequently damaged solidarity. He helped to provoke the German Government into demanding a European withholding tax. He damaged the eurobond market itself by acting as a guiltily uncomplaining recipient of bonds that were not as sound as they might have been. More generally, anonymous coupons also facilitated money laundering. A market aided by a moral compass to its strategic direction would not have tolerated this cancerous criminal component.

There was of course good as well as bad. For example, it was easily able to prevent a massive market collapse in Latin America that would essentially have been based on fraud purporting to be denominated in one currency but in fact denominated in a much softer one. Even so, I recall no occasion when the market's leading operators improved market governance by any reference to ethical considerations.

This lack of behavioural restraint was compounded by the fact that the Eurobond market was deliberately regulated at a level that was substantially less strict than the USA's regulation.

On top of that, there was no shortage of solicitors to give Eurobond practitioners "helpful" advice as to what the very edge of what the law purportedly allowed. There is obvious danger in too rapidly driving, inadequately sighted, along what may or may not be the very edge of a mountain road.

Here are four possible remedies:

1.   International flows of capital are *prima facie* good, not bad. They must operate in a demonstrably effective and pertinent international framework of regulation and that framework must at least be compatible with sound moral purpose if the market is to be sustainable. It is very difficult to see, for example, how London could expect to manage capital surpluses from Islamic countries in the absence of at least a nod in the direction of Sharia financial principles. In fact, the legal framework of Europe's financial

systems and the demands of sovereign borrowers, while in themselves secular, should at least be demonstrably compatible with generic Abrahamic traditions and genuine and measurable environmental sustainability. Even if such parameters appeared to pinch short term rates of return on capital, which I do not believe is by any means inevitable, perhaps associated limitations on behaviour might help to give less weight to delinquent mindsets and to limit excessive market volatility. In the absence of its historic overwhelming military power, Europe must offer the best products and one ingredient is ethical reliability;

2. Rating agencies have had the prerogative of the harlot throughout the ages: power without responsibility. Robust rating is essential to bring sufficient transparency to markets to enable investors to make reasonably informed decisions. Europe needs at least one rating agency of unimpeachable integrity and competence: a hard nut, not a soft touch. In an era of international capital flows, rating agencies must themselves be subject to a rigorous and specialist global regulator. The more complex the products on offer, the greater the need for this vital reform;

3. Single markets require co-ordinated regulation. The EU's financial services markets should synthesise the best Europe has to offer: this best will have a more Anglo-German than "Anglo Saxon" character. Those of us who thought about market and regulatory structures nearly twenty years ago would have been astonished and dismayed if we had known that, in 2008, Europe would still lack its own effective financial services regulator. Such a regulator would not be the complete solution: it would need, in a context of the global capital flows that can best serve Europe's interest, much better integration into an effective system of global regulation reflecting today's global balance of economic power;

4. The UK is likely to emerge from the recession with a potentially vicious circle of relatively high interest rates and inflation and a weak currency, which uncorrected over

time would lead to 1970s style stagflation with, however, no prospect of return to the glory days of massive revenues from North Sea oil. But Britain's Post War spiv society – of which inflation and devaluation were always part - has run its course with this business cycle. In a context where its economic weight is lower than before, the UK will be only one of many possible vigorously competing destinations – and already more indebted than most - for surplus overseas savings, a pressure that will require from us progressively more sustainable and stable monetary policy aligned with the bulk of the European single market.

The British Government will find itself, after a generation of deliberate de-industrialisation, more dependent than ever on the contribution of international financial services to GDP and enjoying much less freedom of manoeuvre than in earlier cycles. Challenge, however, always brings opportunity. Revitalising the City's credibility as Europe's financial capital, and over time, stabilising and re-balancing the rest of the British economy, will increasingly be seen in a context of demographic change to be linked to the longer term reliability of the store of value of the local currency. There will be a tipping point for British public opinion: with a fair wind, the UK will enter the Euro at a relatively soft rate and then progressively adjust to monetary conditions which re-stabilise prices and healthy real rates of return on invested capital. London has an opportunity to build the World's most sustainable capital market, global in reach but based on a single, shared, strong currency and reflecting shared European values.

Dirk Hazell - The first European General Counsel and Compliance Director of Daiwa Securities. Formerly an arbitrator at the SFA and Director of IPMA. Now CEO of the Environmental Services Association. A barrister.

Time to be Brave…

Economic arguments for and against any given course of action are never unambiguous. The list of pluses will always be offset by some minuses – and all are subject to enormous uncertainty. It is not just that we are dealing with known and unknown unknowns that making forming a judgement very hard. On top there is no failsafe economic theory either to interpret the present or predict the future.

So it is with the Euro. One of the difficulties of the way the argument against British membership has been pitched in Britain is that opponents see no pluses whatsoever. It is a long list of minuses. Countries need independent currencies in order to manage economic shocks, argue the antis. The economic rules in the Euro zone are rigid. The European Central Bank is unaccountable. The Euro is not going to work in the medium term. There are already enormous strains between member states reflected in credit default swap rates that vary hugely between countries. There is no central fiscal authority. Britain needs the pound to fall as a key part of its adjustment to the credit crunch and recession; being locked in a single currency would be fatal. And anyway why should Britain want to lose its proud currency and sink its identity and destiny with Europeans?

Some of these arguments are telling, but all have powerful rejoinders. And all of them presuppose that Britain is doing fine outside the Euro and can continue to have a perfectly viable economic future. It is this last proposition that is increasingly difficult to maintain, especially after the events of the last twelve months. There are major questions to answer about how Britain's economic structure is to develop in future, how in particular we are to manage the enormous risks associated with having bank assets that have grown to more than four times our GDP and whether the world is evolving in such a way that being outside rather than inside a major currency and trading block is rational. These are big questions – and which the antis singularly fail to address.

My contention is that Euro membership must be considered as a strategic option that will allow Britain both to sustain its lucrative role as an international financial centre and boost its knowledge intensive manufacturing and service sectors. It would place Britain at the heart of what is emerging as a major currency block, and which will increasingly shape the world's international financial system. It will offer a stability and predictability in both currency and interest rates that is much needed by British business, particularly as the current exchange rate would "lock" in a reasonable rate that has not been the case over decades of capital inflows and petro-status. And although there are advantages in having a floating exchange rate they are rapidly diminishing. These are important gains that cannot be put to one side.

The antis have never come to terms with the likelihood and now reality of the Euro's success. When the Euro launched 10 years ago, an unnamed Euro-sceptic currency trader - now almost certainly redundant - famously called it a toilet currency. In recent months it has been climbing to record highs against both the pound and dollar. Eurozone countries are key actors in the discussions about reshaping the world monetary system. Yet in Britain the mainstream consensus remains that the Euro is about to fall apart.

One piece of damning evidence is that the market prices the likelihood of default on Greek, Italian and Portuguese national debt (all denominated in Euro) as very much higher than, say, German or French debt. Credit default swap rates are telling us, they crow, that the system has irresolvable tensions. They never, never draw attention to the varying credit default swaps on American municipal bonds – the risk premium between Californian and Texan debt is as large – even larger – than the gap between Greek and German. The market is simply acknowledging risk – but the risk in both the Euro and dollar area is not that the monetary regime is about to collapse. It is that particular borrowers are overborrowed.

Another is that the banking crisis has underlined that the Euro is a currency in search of a fiscal authority – vital for banking crises and to ensure that the total volume of Euro denominated public debt does not swamp the market as governments lose control of their finances. Yet the co-ordinated response of the Eurozone countries to the necessary recapitalisation of their banks has shown that the system can manage without a centralised fiscal authority. Indeed there are virtues in particular jurisdictions - like Ireland or Luxembourg – having to confront the reality of their own policy decisions in following Iceland in developing an overlarge financial sector. The rules on the level and rate of public borrowing are tough, but they are flexible – particularly in emergencies as at present. Both Spain and France are budgeting for deficits in 2009 that exceed the 3 per cent of GDP permitted maximum. It is true that neither approach the projected British level of 8 per cent, but Britain entered the downturn with a structural deficit that was between 2 to 3 per cent of GDP too high. Some discipline on British public finances, and some credible rules about how Britain is to manage its finances in future having necessarily abandoned the framework developed by Gordon Brown as Chancellor, is now vitally necessary. The Euro provides such a framework.

I write as a Keynesian who believes in the need for discretionary fiscal policy. But Keynesianism, as I have argued from more than twenty five years, is not a philosophy of big and never-ending budget deficits. It is about a system of managing finance and financial markets that destabilise the operation of the real economy. Fiscal policy is a crucial but not sole element in the equation. The structure and disciplines of the international financial system are indispensable (hence the Keynesian case for fixed exchange rates internationally). So is monetary policy. So are quantitative, administrative and structural measures to boost or constrain the growth of credit. And if fiscal policy is to be activist, it must also be conducted within a credible system of long term rules.

Seen through this prism the Euro is more Keynesian than its critics acknowledge – notwithstanding the importance it attaches to money supply measures and inflation as part of the European Central Bank's legacy from the Bundesbank. The Euro manages the relationship between the Eurozone and the rest of the world in a way that would be impossible if there were a patchwork quilt of different European currencies. The European Central Bank has demonstrated a welcome willingness to deploy the full array of quantitative and administrative measures to underwrite the European banking system as a whole during the crisis that otherwise would have been wilting. If different nation states had responded differently with different currency regimes, there would almost certainly have been a domino effect with the best being only as strong as the weakest. When the history of the current financial crisis is written, one of the mitigating factors will have been the existence of the Euro.

Critics make much of the vital necessity of Britain having discretion over its economic policy because of its particularities and need to adjust. But those particularities – notably an overblown financial system that is four and half times the size of our GDP – are not necessarily particularities we should cherish. It is true that the devaluation of the pound has been an important adjustment mechanism, but the "thank god we were outside the Euro because the current crisis would only be worse "school needs challenging. Interest rates would have been lower, it is true, which alone would have made the housing market even more buoyant. But fiscal policy would have been considerably tighter, and financial regulation would have been tougher at the margins. And the concerns now that beset British policy, and indeed the future of the economy and the pound which add to its weakness, would be less

For whatever the pros and cons of membership ten years ago, the argument is about now after a major depreciation in the pound. Britain is "Iceland on Thames". It is the City's need to borrow at least £100bn a year for the foreseeable future, on top of the government's need to borrow the same - made acutely more difficult by a sterling crisis - that is the heart of the crisis of confidence. Suddenly membership of the Euro - politically toxic - is beginning to look a very attractive escape route. Britain may muddle through. The fall in the pound will stimulate exports and, if it does not become a rout, it is welcome. But there is a real danger that in a country that currently resembles a gigantic hedge fund, the fall could get out of hand. The foreign savers on whom the government and banks rely to finance their debts went on strike 12 months ago. Now they are actively withdrawing their cash. One of the US's top banks, the Bank of New York Mellon, recently revealed that in September and October of 2008, three quarters of the capital that foreigners had brought into Britain in the preceding four years had left - more than £100bn.

What worries them is that with plunging property values, the viability of British banks remains questionable, but the UK government has not got a deep enough pocket to bail them out again. British savings are inadequate. If a company gets into this situation it declares bankruptcy because it has not the cash to continue trading. If foreign cash continues to leave, the UK faces the same fate.

However, bankruptcy works differently for a country; it spells economic stagnation. The ardent hope is that this does not happen. If investors start to consider the pound cheap and endorse the government's handling of the economy, they may start buying sterling assets again. But suppose the worst happens, what then?

There is the Latin American option. Instead of trying to sell bonds, the government would simply instruct the Bank of England effectively to print money. It may want to do this anyway if deflation looms, but now its hand would be forced. But once on this path there is no easy way back; savers and investors are crowded out by the printing press and the country gets locked in a cycle of inflation in a broken-backed economy with an angry, rapidly impoverished middle class.

The next option is to organise a jumbo - up to $200bn - loan from the IMF, EU and US to tide the economy over. The Europeans and Americans would both insist that Britain negotiate a deal with the IMF as the precondition for the loan. It would be a re-run of Labour Chancellor Denis Healey turning to the IMF in April 1976 - only now it would be Alistair Darling and Gordon Brown. One insider, contemplating the prospect, acknowledged it would be political suicide.

The last, best and most palatable option is to join the Euro, and fight a referendum campaign on it being our get-out-of-jail-free card - a means of avoiding de facto national bankruptcy and emasculation of the property-owning middle class while offering a route to reindustrialisation and underwriting the City of London. Inside the Euro, both the government and the City would be able to use Euro borrowing within a disciplined framework as a bridge to a more sustainable future. The competitive level at which we would join would boost industrial exports for a generation. And the middle class would not have its savings wrecked by inflation. We would avoid the clutches of the IMF.

Importantly, at the moment, the five tests for entry set by Gordon Brown are all met. Britain and Europe's economies are in perfect synch as we enter recession simultaneously. The labour market is flexible. Entry would attract much-needed inward investment, and support the otherwise dangerously threatened City. It would boost growth. In economic and political terms it would be a masterstroke. Britain would become a member of a reserve currency zone at a competitive level, offering us a key role in the emergent debate about the governance of globalisation and the international financial system. We would remain prosperous and we would matter.

The more open question is whether the Eurozone countries would have us. Part of the admissions process would be offering tough commitments on public spending and borrowing. Equally we would have to commit to manage the pound within a certain range up to the point of entry, and Eurozone countries would be as anxious for the rate to be higher as we would be to lock in today's advantageous rate. The negotiations would be fraught. But the resulting commitments would give a credibility to policy that may yet be vitally necessary before the crisis is over – and which is lacking in the current framework.

Of course there are risks to membership. We lose power over interest rates – but that power is vastly overstated. British interest rates move in synch with European and American rates. We would lose the power to devalue – but we gain the advantage of long run stability at a competitive rate. We would have to work more hand in glove with fellow Europeans to manage our economy, forcing us to recognise our European-ness and to develop institutions that will help us re-industrialise rather than become blind adherents to the American Business Model. I would welcome the opportunity.

But there is no denying the toxicity of the issue in British politics, or how much brave political leadership it will require. There is a vocal and influential part of our country that is against Europe on any terms. They cheerleaded Britain into becoming a de facto hedge fund in the name of free markets. They would now rather risk endemic inflation or endless recession and stagnation to avoid the dark hand of Europe. They are not only bullies. On the balance of the arguments they are wrong.

121
Will Hutton

Will Hutton - Executive Vice Chair of The Work Foundation, professorial fellow at the LSE and regular columnist for the Observer. He has written a number of books including "The State We're In", "The Writing on the Wall" and "The World We're In".

Should Britain Join the Euro: A Lesson from History

The scale and nature of the recent crash in the financial markets is leading to a rethink of the present model of economics and regulation. Can it really be tolerable, people are asking, for such risks to be taken by a banking system that, if those risks go bad, cannot possibly make good the losses itself?

Those few voices that asked that question during the recent period of growth have been joined by many more now that those risks have visibly started to go wrong. It is too early to say precisely what new regulatory framework might be established in place of the

Richard Laming

discredited old model, but the changes are likely to be far-reaching. The failure of the present model has been so comprehensive.

This is a question that will be asked around the world, but there is another question that needs to be asked in the United Kingdom. For the UK has seen not merely a failure of its economic regulation, but of its whole national economic strategy.

For while the crash may have started in America and while it may have spread around the world, its effects have not been felt equally everywhere. The British economy has been much more badly hit than most.

For evidence of this, one need look no further than the exchange rate. Since the problems of the American mortgage market first started to emerge in August 2007, the pound has sharply lost nearly 30 per cent of its value against the Euro (falling from 1.48 to 1.12). This is a devaluation on an almost unprecedented scale. (There is a single example of a sterling devaluation greater than this, to which we will return). And devaluations matter.

Traditional economic theory tells us that the exchange rate should vary according to the balance of payments, so that a country that imports more than it exports should see its exchange rate fall so as to offset the value. In an era of floating exchange rates, this process should happen gradually and seamlessly. Instead, we have seen a sudden and dramatic loss of value, which must have a cause other than simply the balance of payments.

That cause is the failure of Britain's economic strategy.

Britain's economic strategy has been to stand aside from the main project of European integration, namely the Euro, and its notions of modestly balanced budgets and prudent financial regulation, and instead to cast itself as an offshore commercial paradise, founded on a mountain of unsustainable debt.

Regulations and business costs were kept low; the exchange rate and disposable incomes were high. House prices became the measure of economic success. The regulators did not care that for every family that benefited from an increase in the value of the home they lived in, another family could not make even the first rung on the housing ladder. Personal indebtedness rose to record levels to fund more and more extravagant lifestyles. It was an economic strategy that felt like success.

But eventually, as bubbles will, that bubble burst. We can now see that those indications of prosperity were like the thirteenth strike of the clock. Not only do we not believe it, we now realise that the clock was faulty during its previous twelve strikes.

We should reject the assertion that the British economic model did well during the past 10 years up until the crash. The European balance of power kept the peace very well until June 1914, after all.

No, it is not possible to separate the good times from the bad times that those good times subsequently caused. It is not wise to make a car faster by removing its brakes.

It cannot be coincidence that the British recession is so bad compared to those of the Germans or the French: it derives directly from the way we have viewed the world and our place in it. Our national strategy has let us down.

We have been here before.

In the late 1940s, Britain laboured under the delusion that, having been a victorious power in the Second World War, it could now separate itself from the fate of the rest of Europe. It imagined that its place as one of the Big Three at the wartime conferences could be continued in perpetuity, but of course it could not.

In a vain bid to remain a superpower, Britain maintained its military spending and overseas deployments at levels far in excess of what it could afford and out of all proportion to the threats it really faced. Hundreds of thousands of soldiers were deployed in the Middle East and in South East Asia. Britain was even preparing for possible war with the Soviet Union without reference to what the Americans might do.

The military delusion was matched by an economic one. It was hoped that sterling could continue to play a role as a reserve currency, but that would require Britain to act as importer of last resort for the countries in the sterling area. For a country that was struggling even to pay for its own imports, to intervene on behalf of other countries was too much to hope for.

A loan obtained from the Americans of $3.75 billion and later Marshall Aid of $2.7 billion were not enough to solve the problem, merely postpone it.

Such a national strategy could be paid for only by a substantial growth in UK foreign debts and, ultimately, it led to devaluation on an unprecedented scale in 1949, when the pound was reduced from $4.03 to $2.80. This fall of 30.5 per cent has not been matched since then, except – ominously – today.

As with the 1940s, there has been a mismatch between Britain's national strategy and Britain's underlying resources. A common thread was the mistaken belief that our economic health and our place in the world could somehow be separated from those of our European neighbours.

Unlike in the 1940s, we cannot look to the Americans for a financial bail-out. They have been labouring under equivalent economic and strategic misjudgements of their own. We have to strike out on a new course, and join the Euro.

The bad news is that a recession is the wrong time to join a new currency bloc. It is necessary to find an exchange rate between the pound and the Euro that can be sustained forever, and there is far too much uncertainty in the markets to be able to that with confidence. The European treaties require a minimum of two years before such an exchange rate can be settled upon: two years' hence Britain will still be in recession, so the process of joining will not be quick.

Furthermore, it will be hard to keep the public deficit below the stipulated level of 3 per cent of GDP. The government's forecasts predict that that figure will be exceeded for every year between now and 2013, and let us hope that they are not overoptimistic.

But the economic questions of convergence can be solved, if the political decision is taken. And it is indeed a political decision. Joining the Euro is not a simple matter of economic policy, but a choice of national strategy. There is more to it than simply reprinting the banknotes. It requires a new approach to the global economy and Britain's place in it. It leaves behind the delusions and mismanagements of the past, and offers instead the consolidation of British economic interests into an effective financial framework.

To joining the Euro will take a number of years to achieve, but the time for political preparation is now.

The government failed to fix the roof while the sun was shining, but that does not mean that the country should simply accept the rain. There is an umbrella under which Britain can shelter: it is called the Euro.

Richard Laming - Director of Federal Union and Secretary of the European Movement.

Let's Save the Pound – Make it the Euro-Pound

If recent trends continue the pound may fall further to reach parity with the Euro.

Even the most chauvinist of Britons – however sceptical they have been about the Euro and all its works - will be somewhat equivocal about it falling below parity – the Euro having started life at 1 January 1999 with the pound worth €1. 52, i.e. the Euro was worth 66 pence. Now (late-December 2008) the pound is worth only €1.05, the Euro being worth 95 pence.

129
David Lea

One reason why the financial crisis and the recession has hit the value of the US dollar and the pound has been the role of financial services in their country's economic structure - then after the banking collapse, the necessary huge fiscal expansion and issue of more government bonds.

UK Policy

Let us list three largely incontrovertible facts:

(i) "Join the Euro when the five economic tests have been met" is still government policy.
(ii) The five tests have been met.
(iii) Ergo, await an early government announcement.

Or perhaps not. The five tests seem to be a moveable feast rather than – as one had assumed – a periodic examination. But the unstated objection is the Catch 22 that
(a) we won't win a referendum, so
(b) we can't start a campaign,   so
(c) we are stuck where we are.

But equally, the world has changed irrevocably – and I will spell out why this frozen politics is absurd, now that economics has been unfrozen in such a spectacular way.

We cannot – if we are to look further than the end of our noses (which most people refuse to do) refuse to look again at all our options. Far from "talking the pound down", what we are advocating is that **now is the time to consider the modalities of fixing the rate.** It is our opponents who view regular devaluations with equanimity.

The tenth anniversary of the setting up of the Eurozone and fixing the rate is of course also the tenth anniversary of the last serious debate in this country – not just among politicians but industry and trade unionists, the media, the retail trade, financial services, manufacturing and tourism - in all the regions of Britain. But like Rip van Winkle, we have had our head firmly under the pillow ever since.

Gordon Brown's 1999 speech to the TUC

The year 1999 also marks the high point – so far – of Gordon Brown's enthusiasm. It is opportune on this anniversary to revisit his overview at that time – conveniently set out in the **annexed** speech he made at a TUC Conference in May 1999 on "Unions and the Euro".

In his words: "We are the first government to state that there is no overriding constitutional barrier to membership" (page 5 of his speech) It is in this connection that Gordon Brown's characterisation of the political economy of the eurozone is worth quoting in full:
"Their macro economic stability is to be pursued through monetary union ... through a single currency, intended as it does to remove unnecessary currency speculation within Europe, to reduce transaction costs which are a barrier and a big expense to business often at the expense to employment ... We are the first British government to declare for the principle of that currency union"

Devaluation and Stability

The central dimension of stability is undoubtedly the exchange rate with the rest of the economic area in which we carry out most of our trade –and that of course is the European economic area, in which European, including British, multinationals make most of their living.

The mantra repeated ad nauseam by such commentators as Martin Wolf in the Financial Times that the opportunity to devalue must be preserved as an essential policy option - the central rationale of their mindset – reflects the fact that they are fighting a fundamentalist war in defence of some imagined Anglo- American economic Magisterium. It is the American model of capitalism (not necessarily President Obama's version but that is another story) which is central to their dogma – they far prefer this to the social market capitalism of the EU. And it is the EU model rather than US model which is starting to win that argument, not least because of the nemesis of the capital markets in recent weeks.

Exchange rate stability – and the removal of the transaction costs inside that zone and attendant currency movements (these can be hedged against but that is still an unnecessary barrier) - does of course in one respect beg the question of the correct rate at which to join.

It is worth noting that the rate today - when one Euro equals about 95 pence at the time of writing - might not be the rate available in two years time, any more than the rate of roughly 66 pence to the € in January 1999 persisted. Looking at it the other way round, we have now slipped a long way towards parity with the Euro; and if we want to stop in our tracks before that then we need an action plan to do something about it.

Industry is not looking for a lower rate than parity; it is now looking for some stability - and this logically extends to mutual support for reserves at certain exchange rates - though this has not been openly talked about so far.

It is sometimes said that the UK's ejection from the exchange rate mechanism in 1992 is a convincing argument for not going into the Eurozone. In fact, of course, as even Lord Lamont would I think accept, these are two totally different and non- comparable scenarios if fixing the rate at parity amounts to us entering the waiting room to the Euro.

Moreover, Britain would of course now have a much more significant role in the European Economic Area if a full member of the Eurozone, which looks likely to cover 80 or 90% of all the 27 member states within a few years - with a huge share of our exports and investments and likewise imports and inward investments.

Norway and Switzerland are often referred to as paragons of virtue for staying outside the EU and the Euro. But they are hardly role models. There are special balance of payments reasons for their position, in connection with oil and gas and financial services respectively. Also among the remarkable features which these two alpine countries share is the statistic that whereas each cow in the EU is subsidised by about $200 a year, the equivalent figure in Norway and Switzerland is about $1,000.

EU/China/USA

When in the mid 70's the basket of European currencies was first established – subsequently to become the basis of the Euro – its initial setting was equal to a dollar; now of course it is worth about $1.40. This is not surprising in view of the astronomical United States trade deficit with China, sustained - until recently - only by huge Chinese reciprocal investments in US companies and real estate; and also by treating the dollar as a reserve currency. That is now showing signs of rapid unwinding and the Euro is a beneficiary.

What is the UK's alternative to the Euro in terms of credible currency zones? Now in particular is not the time to try and become the 51st State of the USA - or of China come to that. The depth of our involvement in the EU - the growing extent of our integration - means that the leadership recently shown by Gordon Brown on the bank recapitalisation and on the coordinated fiscal stimulus -is part of a further move forward for the EU as a whole. This is not to deny that the circumstances are extraordinarily difficult of all of us in the EU and we cannot expect perfection in coordination, though crocodile tears for any deficiencies are not in order either...

Any European industrial policy in which we would be engaged would have to be concerted in the EU Council; in other words, the EU would need to reach agreement about temporary industrial support in the recession; and increase the role of the European Investment Bank - and national bodies in parallel - and the European Globalisation Adjustment Fund, to assist with redundancies and restructuring.

The Standing of the Euro

Other factors have not stood still. The widespread UK scepticism in 1999 about how the Euro would fare has been largely replaced by the recognition that the ECB has become a highly respected institution and currency - indeed for India and China it is increasingly a candidate for the status of a reserve currency alongside - or in substitution for - the US dollar.

Familiarity with the Euro is now self- reinforcing in Africa, Asia and Latin America as well as in the OECD area. The pound is nowhere by comparison.

So the doomsayers' mantra of "it won't work" - mutating through to "it will, but it will entail the demise of proud European nations like France and Germany" - often appearing in the same speech - are seen for what they are in large part - parochial prejudice mixed with imperial nostalgia and condescension. In any event, to define the issue in terms of patriotism is a bit rich when one reflects on the history of relations between France and Germany and the cement which Europe provides in that relationship.

Jobs and Inward Investment

More substantial is the issue of pay and jobs... Of course, this debate begs the question as to whether a slide in the pound protects real pay rates in the medium term or not. What has been proved to be accurate was the point made by the TUC in 1999, that if the Euro entry delay persisted for a period of years Britain would become a less attractive place relatively for inward investments. This moment of truth this is now evident from the latest statistics, and we are now in danger of being in the worst of both worlds. Moreover, it is at EU level that we can make the quickest progress in securing accountability and taxation transparency of multinational businesses, including multinational banks and associated new financial instruments.

As Gordon Brown concluded in 1999 "to withdraw from Europe or go outside Europe's mainstream and become a sort of "Hong Kong" of Europe, a low wage competitor with the Far East or some sort of dream of a tax haven servicing major trading blocks - the idea that Britain was some sort of greater Guernsey - only needs a minute's consideration to be rejected".

The Euro and the Recession

How does all this stack up against the present economic crisis? Easing fiscal rules to deal with the recession is being sanctioned by the Council of Ministers, and this is the answer to those who argued that the European Union Economic Policy would be dominated by a deflationary Central Bank Policy. Clearly there is a debate involving in particular France and Germany about the effect of picking up other people's bills but there has also been an increase of Community solidarity, albeit it on the tried and tested basis of "two steps forward, one step back".

The current crisis in Greece has, no doubt, specific local features but it reminds us inter alia that structural change in a recession can create huge tensions in regard to social factors such as jobs for youth and income distribution. But the Euro is - notwithstanding that - a positive rather than a negative factor - a necessary condition but by no means a sufficient condition - and the same is true for other weaker economies. Speculation against the drachma, for example, could by now have reached catastrophic proportions.

The Social Dimension

Another consideration for people at work - strongly endorsed by Gordon Brown in his address in 1999 and proven by events - is that the Social Chapter has been a great advance for people at work and has not been at the expense of levels of employment. Agreed by the social partners in Brussels - in which the TUC has played a significant role, along with colleagues in the ETUC and the European Parliament, many of the specific measures had been introduced earlier on the Continent and were implemented in the UK only when then the Labour government signed up in 1997.

It is an impressive list: European Works Councils (1994), Maternity and Parental Leave (1992/1996); Health and Safety Standards (from 1989). Cross- frontier Posting of Workers (1996) Rights to Information and Consultation (2002/05/07), pro rata Rights for Fixed-term Contract workers (2002), ditto Part time workers (1997) and Temporary/Agency workers (2008); Four weeks paid holiday (1993/ 2001/05).

Earlier enactments such has the Transfer of Undertakings (Protection of Employment Rights) Regulations (1977) and that on Collective Redundancies (1970) go back so far in time that people can forget that they too emanated for then EU, as did Equal Pay (1975); and regulations on Sex Discrimination (1976). Imagine the "Competitiveness" objection if we had tried to do these things on our own.

Measurement of real income growth, wage and productivity comparisons is less ambiguous within the currency zone and although working hours have to be taken into consideration, there is now very little to choose between any of what one might call the Northern European group of economies covering two thirds of Europe's output - with some differences with the Mediterranean countries and Eastern Europe. But the very fact that the central core of economies have very similar structures and levels of productivity is the answer of those people who had forecast that the system would collapse; on the contrary, it is other systems of which that might more truthfully be said.

Timescale - Prepare and Decide

In his 1999 speech the then Chancellor spoke of the five economic tests as paramount but some Ministers may be tempted to argue that this is now more about the politics. **But we cannot keep chopping and changing now that the five tests have been met - as other contributions to this report demonstrate.**

So to conclude with a particularly apposite remark by Gordon Brown in his speech of May 1999 "Our view has been that, instead of the old wait and see attitude which came from the last government, we must make the preparations which are necessary to allow us to make a genuine decision , subject to a referendum of the people of this country. **So our policy is not "wait and see" but "prepare and decide"**

The Euro-Pound Area

So it is now overdue to set out a road map, including a preliminary question which ought even to attract the support of William Hague: **"Do you want to save the £ by stopping it falling below parity with the €?" I think the answer would be positive. People from all classes in the community can see their well - earned foreign holidays costing more; and that the countries they go to are not generally falling behind us but in many cases catching up.**

The Murdoch press cannot fool all of the people all of the time. And many of those politicians who say they support devaluation today would very quickly identify themselves as the *same* **politicians who would cry crocodile tears for the country's plight - and try and make political capital out of it - if the pound fell below parity.**

The opportunity may well arise for us to fix the £/€ rate at parity, though that too would need a joint preparation with our partners. That half-way-house would then - de facto - be the first step towards joining, as it would mean that we were - in essentials - part of the Euro–Pound Area.

In celebrating the real achievements of the Euro on its 10th anniversary on New Year's Day, we need to part company with the conventional wisdom which suggests that this is all too much of a political nightmare. On the contrary, the British people are renowned for their respect for - and acceptance of - pragmatic step-by-step approaches to solving problems - in particular when the concept has been tried and tested over 10 years.

David Lea - Assistant General Secretary TUC 1977-99. Vice President ETUC 1994-99; Treasury Advisory Group on the Euro 1998-99.

The Benefits of Euro Area Membership from a Purely Economic Perspective

There are many arguments brought against Euro membership in the UK. In this short essay I want to focus on a single argument, according to which the benefits of a fit-to-measure monetary policy outweigh the economic advantages of Euro membership, such as improvements in trade integration, greater resistance to global shocks, and potentially lower real interest rates.

I myself would grant that, all other thing being equal, the UK was better off staying outside during the first ten years of the Euro. When I say this, I assume that the UK would have pursued a similar

Wolfang Munchau

fiscal policy under a hypothetical Euro regime – perhaps marginally tighter, as the fiscal stance would have been subject to criticisms from the EU Commission and other Euro area member states. In terms of financial regulation, I would not expect Euro membership to have made any difference. With an interest rate gap of around 1 percentage point, the UK credit bubble would have been much worse than it already was. The housing bubble would also have been more extreme, perhaps aided by Euro area capital inflows as currency risk is removed. In a scenario in which all other things are equal, almost all economic problems the UK has had over the last few years – property bubble, credit bubble, unsustainably high current account deficit, insufficiently high savings rate – would have been even worse with the Euro.

Of course, things may not have been the same. If the British government had tightened fiscal policy, or adopted a more conservative regulatory framework for mortgages, for example by encouraging more long-term lending, some of these problems could have been avoided. But I suspect that the UK would not have undertaken those policy changes, and for that reason I am happy to state that the UK was indeed better off staying outside.

But I expect economic circumstance to change in such a profound way that it will affect the assessment of the relative benefits. Let me try to give a sense of what I expect to happen over the next ten years. For a start, the UK has to find some other specialization than finance, and redefine its concept of a modern service economy. I personally never found the distinction of services and manufacturing very useful, especially not in an age when many of those functions are intertwined. I find a taxonomy on the basis of skills and innovative capacity more useful, and while I would admit that Germany cares too much about the car industry, I see no evidence at all that the UK outperforms continental European economies in terms of innovation – other than so-called financial innovation, which is the opposite of innovation.

So how will the financial crisis affect this balance? For our debate in particular, it will have two profound long-term implications. The appetite for another housing bubble is seriously constrained for a long time to come, and regulation is almost certain to be set up to hinder a repeat of a bubble. Mortgage finance will in future be much more strictly controlled, possibly with externally set limits for mortgage advances, relative to the price of the house, and the applicant's income. Given time, central banks will also find a way to take house prices into account when setting monetary policy, and I would expect that after the house price decline is over (my estimate is for a total peak-to-trough fall of 40-50% in both the US and the UK), real prices will stagnate or grow at moderate levels for a long time.

The death of the shadow banking system will be a seminal shock for the City of London, which had most recently specialized in the seedier end of the credit market. The City will remain Europe's most important financial centre, but this will not mean much in economic terms. (It is like having the tallest building, or the longest river, of importance mainly to quiz shows). Of course, the financial sector fulfils important economic functions, and will do so in the future, but then so do taxis and dry cleaners. But they are not worth 8 per cent of GDP, as this is the case with UK finance.

I would also expect the era of global free-floating exchange rate to come to an end slowly. Recent research has indicated that free floating exchange rates have not aided current account adjustment, as its advocates had always argued. I do not want to launch into a broader discussion of future global exchange rate regime, but I am confident to predict that there will be more management of exchange rates, and less complacency about huge current account imbalances.

In Europe, I would expect that accession to the eurozone to continue, and gather speed. All of East Europe EU will join the Euro, as will Denmark. Iceland will join the EU, as well as Euro, if and when the country meets the criteria.

This is the environment in respect of which we have to judge the question of the relative benefits of independent currency at the fringes of the Euro area. In this environment, I would expect more exchange rate volatility between the remaining exchange rate blocks, as volatility is reduced inside those blocks. The UK would almost certainly experience periods of intense exchange rate volatility, as it gets caught between those blocks, and this will deter investors.

As a consequence of this, but also because of doubts about domestic fiscal policy and the long-term solvency of the state, investors will demand higher risk premiums. Of course, entering the Euro does not make you any more solvent, but investors are crucially facing a different risk. If you default all on your own, like Argentina or Iceland, the result is a total bloodbath, possibly threatening the survival of the state. If you were to default as a member of a large currency zone, the process would be far more orderly. You still have a financial and an economic crisis, but at least you won't have a currency crisis to deal with as well.

UK sovereign risk spreads are already going up in the credit default swap market. With its large exposure to the financial sector, the UK shares some similarities with Iceland. The UK is thus hugely vulnerable to a speculative attack, which in turn drives up risk premiums.

I would also expect immigration flows to reverse. The Poles are already returning. And if the UK ceases to be a quick bang-for-the-buck economy over longer periods of time, then it becomes a lot less attractive for foreigners to invest here. If the City of London is cut down to size, expect those masses of continental Europeans and Americans who flocked to live in London in recent years to return home.

Monetary policy would also face huge hurdles in this environment. To remain credible from a policy standpoint, the Bank of England would have to maintain its current inflation target framework through thick and thin. As the economy weakens, the Bank will surely relax monetary policy, and this would be fine initially. But if and when the economy finally emerges from the crisis, one should expect a very dramatic tightening of monetary conditions to mop up all the excess liquidity provided during the crisis. This can be done, of course, but it will pose a serious constraint on economic growth for quite some time.

Without the help of permanently cheap interest rates, a housing and a financial bubble, I cannot see how the UK economy can generate the high rates of growth the country got used to over the last 10 years. This is going to prove a much more difficult environment for monetary policy than those 15 years of the Great Moderation, during which globalization put pressure on inflation rates everywhere. In other words, an independent monetary policy may not turn out to be advantageous at all. Real and nominal interest rates are going to be higher than in the Euro area, and the central bank is more likely to miss the target in such an environment. Joining the Euro would provide a much more stable economic framework.

This process could go so far that the benefits of an independent monetary regime would be negative. When that happens, you no longer talk about a trade-off between the benefits of an independent currency regime, and the membership of monetary union. In that case, you want to adopt precisely because you actually want to get rid of the pound and the independent Bank of England. (It will still be independent, but it will be part of another central banking system).

To summarise, I expect the external situation to change so dramatically, that the benefits of staying out, while real in the past, will completely disappear. I also suspect that this change of economic fortunes will ultimately be reflected by public opinion.

Wolfgang Munchau - Associate Editor and columnist of the Financial Times. One of the founding members of Financial Times Deutschland, where he served as deputy editor (1999 to 2001), and as editor-in-chief (2001 to 2003). His latest German-language book Vorbeben, about the financial crisis, has received the 2008 Get Abstract book award.

Joining the Euro –
By Rational Decision or Through Crisis?

British ministers have firmly denied that there is any truth to the reported claim by the President of the European Commission, Jose Manuel Barroso, that some "leading political figures" in the government are sufficiently worried about the impact of the economic and financial crisis that they are considering joining the *Euro*. In the light of these denials it is tempting to say that if ministers are not sufficiently worried, then they should be. Virtually every economy in the world will be affected by the global downturn. But the recession is set to hit the UK harder than most other countries and notably harder than those within the Eurozone.

145
John Palmer

At the time of writing, sterling has fallen to record low levels against the Euro on international currency markets. In the context of the world wide capitalist crisis, no one can be confident how much further the pound will lose value against the Euro, nor when nor at what level it will stabilise or when it will eventually go into reverse. What is clear is that a protracted and substantial depreciation of the pound could have a devastating impact on an already badly weakened British economy. A continuing slide in sterling may force UK long term interest rates higher even while the economy is still in the grip of a serious recession.

The present crisis has thrown a devastatingly revealing light on a profound structural imbalance at the heart of the British economy. One measure of this imbalance has been the grossly disproportionate size of the financial services sector within the overall economy. Another is the admittedly long term excessive dependence of the UK economy on the housing market. In Britain as in the case of the United States, the interaction between irresponsibly deregulated and grossly over extended financial services and a suicidal boom in property prices has generated a lethal cocktail.

In none of the Euro-land economies has this distorted pattern been fully repeated, with the possible exception of Ireland. It is true that Ireland and Spain have also suffered from an excessive over investment in housing. But the full impact of these problems has been softened by their participation in European monetary union. Moreover the Spanish regulatory authorities have displayed exemplary judgement in prohibiting some of the worst excesses in the securitisation of debt well before the present crisis.

The recent depreciation of sterling against the Euro has taken place at the same time as a major upward valuation of the dollar against both sterling and the Euro. The dramatic rise in the US dollar appears counter-intuitive in that the United States is running astronomic budget and balance of payments deficits. The explanation has to do with the collapse of US corporate profits which has led to a large scale repatriation of overseas investment back to America to shore up the capital reserves of banks and other financial institutions.

At some point this process will slow down or come to a halt. At that point the dollar will be extremely vulnerable to a worldwide loss of confidence particularly by Asian economies which have traditionally invested their surpluses heavily in US Treasury bills and other assets to offset their vast trade surpluses with the US. But the Chinese and other Asian and Gulf governments have already signalled their intent to diversify their assets and reduce their dependence on holding dollar assets in future.

A full scale US dollar crisis perhaps in 2009 or 2010 would bring with it all manner of negative consequences for a convalescent global financial system. But more immediately, precedent suggests a dollar in free fall would drag sterling down still further with it. It is one thing to argue for sterling to enjoy some competitive advantage in relation to Britain's competitor/partners in the Euro-area. But a collapse of sterling – in the wake of a dollar crisis – but driven also by the mounting indebtedness of the UK governments as a result of its necessary anti-recession crisis measures - could create a nightmare scenario of high long term market interests and the threat of imported inflation while recession still has the economy in its grip.

Little wonder that there is growing discussion about how the British government could insure itself against such an outcome. This discussion in and around official policy making circles may have been one reason why President Barroso has detected some shift in London's attitude to the Euro. But there are other trends which may reinforce a willingness to take up the cause of the Euro. The implosion of the Thatcherite "lightly regulated" economic model is increasing the attractions of the European social model – or more accurately "models" – even for those in the UK who have never been in the pro-European camp.

The Nordic countries, in particular, have demonstrated greater success at balancing economic competitiveness and innovation with far greater social cohesion and prioritisation for environmental sustainability. It is true that, currently, Finland is the only Nordic country fully in the Euro (Denmark is however a full participant in the Exchange Rate Mechanism.) But in both Denmark and Sweden the likelihood is that they will seek to join the single currency in the next year or two. Even traditionally "Euro-sceptic" Icelanders, meanwhile, seem almost desperate to join both the EU and the Euro while Norway could well move in the same direction in the not too distant future.

Of course the domestic political obstacles to joining the Euro in the UK (or more precisely in England) remain formidable. But some recent developments help make the political case for joining the Euro. The first is the flexibility shown over short term implementation of the Maastricht Treaty monetary union disciplines in the context of a serious global recession. It is going to be much harder now for UK Euro-sceptics to present the Euro as a recipe for deflation.

The second helpful trend is precisely the growing attraction of the European social models at a time of economic hardship and acute divisions of wealth and income in Britain. The third has to do with the parallel climate change crisis. The need for Europe as a whole to shift gear profoundly to achieve slower but more environmentally sustainable growth in the decade or so ahead can be cited to justify Britain becoming a full part of the European project. Indeed the costs of remaining a peripheral member of the Union when global economic storms are growing in ferocity can now be made with ever greater confidence. The case for Britain finally becoming part of "core Europe" is vastly strengthened because London is particularly anxious to influence the EU as a whole of the vital issues of CO_2 emissions and climate change.

Of course any change in UK government strategy will require political courage. But it is possible that on this issue – as on others recently – a positive example of constructive engagement with the EU may be set by the devolved administrations in Edinburgh, Cardiff and especially Stormont where the economic fortunes of the north of Ireland are already closely inter-twined with those of the Euro-area Republic.

Naturally a decision in principle to apply to join the Euro would have to be followed by serious negotiations with the Euro-area authorities on the handling of the transition and the need for the UK to fulfil the key criteria for being part of the single currency. Most experts believe that the UK has long since met the "economic tests" set by the present prime minister when Chancellor of the Exchequer for joining the Euro. But the longer the decision is delayed the greater the risk that recent underlying economic convergence between the UK and the Euro-area economies could be put at risk.

It may not be easy to agree an appropriate exchange rate for fixing sterling to the Euro. But it is certainly not in the UK interest to press for a counter-productively low exchange rate. Britain's Euro-area partners will also have an interest in showing constructive flexibility. They know that the Euro-area – and the European Union as a whole – would be politically strengthened by having the UK fully involved. But it is far, far better to begin this process soon while the British government has a reasonably strong bargaining position.

There are then two scenarios which could be imagined for this decisive shift in British state policy. The first is through a rational discussion drawing on the new realities generated by global crisis. The second could be a panic stricken U-turn in policy driven by the crisis when it is at its height. Far better for London to open the debate now while it can make a calm case for joining the Euro, while it is in a position to negotiate terms for fixing the sterling rate against the Euro and while it has some residual influence to shape the future policy strategies of the Euro-area as a whole.

John Palmer – Former Brussels-based European editor of the Guardian (1975 to 2006). Founding Political Director of the European Policy Centre in Brussels (1996 to 2006). Now a leading independent writer and commentator on European affairs.

A Fight We Can Win

Even the most enthusiastic supporter of UK entry to the Euro hedges his bets by saying that public opinion would prevent us adopting the single currency in the foreseeable future, as a referendum could not be won. We should not be so negative.

Only months before the referendum of 1975 on continued membership of the Common Market, polls indicated that the British people were opposed to remaining in by a majority of roughly two to one. Yet the result was almost two to one in favour, a verdict which has done much to help the increasing prosperity of the nation since then.

151
David Seymour

Conditions are not the same now as they were then, of course. In '75, the entire political and media establishment were urging a Yes vote, whereas now not only are the Conservatives utterly hostile to the Euro, but so is much of the media.

But one crucial thing has not changed. The principal reason voters came down on the Yes side in 1975, according to polling by Mori, was that the critical issue on which people decided was the economy. They believed they would be better off inside than out.

In the current economic situation, and as the crisis worsens, voters would decide on the same basis. Issues such as the ability to determine our own interest rates, let alone whether the currency should carry the Queen's head, will become increasingly irrelevant if the UK is perceived as being in a worse situation to deal with the crisis than almost any other country.

During the 2000 Presidential campaign, Bill Clinton's reply to the question, What is this election about, was: 'It's the economy, stupid'. So, as Britain's economic situation becomes ever worse, and the increasingly desperate question is, 'How are we going to get out of this mess?' the answer will be: 'It's the Euro, stupid.'

Already we are in uncharted territory, with bank nationalisation having been accepted virtually overnight as a relevant tool of government policy. So it doesn't require too great a leap of faith to see how a generally hostile British public could quickly come to see membership of the eurozone as being a key step towards restoring stability and prosperity to this country.

But before the people are persuaded, the politicians would have to be. Contrary to some absurd press reports, the Euro is not on the agenda at 10 Downing Street or in the Treasury. So ministers, especially the prime minister and chancellor, would have to accept that they should have the courage of their convictions and take on the blinkered and unremitting antagonism of certain sections of the media.

Once that had been achieved, the campaign to explain how the British people would benefit from membership of the eurozone would have to begin in earnest. It would be politically impossible not to hold a referendum so a major campaign which for the first time explained how much the UK has gained from being in the EU and how we would benefit by adopting the Euro would have to be launched and fought with conviction. Half-hearted campaigning would lead to inevitable, and justifiable, defeat. As the government cannot contemplate that, it must fight with every available weapon to secure victory.

Winning is not as tough as our opponents would have us believe. The reality is that, for most people, antagonism to the Euro (and Europe) is skin deep. Only a small minority – less than 10 per cent, according to the best estimates – are totally opposed, so the vast majority are ready to be persuaded. That will be our task.

There was an interesting example of what can be achieved in the BBC television programme Referendum Street in 2000. The residents of a suburban street were allowed to ballot on whether they thought the UK should go into the Euro or not. The result was a significant No. Then two teams, one on each side, campaigned in the street for a week, before a second ballot was held. This time the result was Yes, by a substantial majority.

This turn-around was due to the Yes team concentrating purely on the economic benefits of membership of the eurozone, while the No side banged on about the Queen's head and a thousand years of the pound sterling.

So I see the greatest obstacle preventing our entry to the Euro being not the people, who can be open-minded towards what is in their best interests, but the politicians, who are scared of a hostile press. It is a remarkable hypocrisy that those newspapers which are most antagonistic towards UK membership of the eurozone are those which complain most loudly that politicians are spineless. Yet there is no issue on which politicians have been more supine than British relations with the EU and, particularly, entry to the Euro.

David Seymour

It is particularly extraordinary that this has happened when such a high proportion of British companies are deeply involved in Europe, as is the City. Those who criticise the government over, for example, attempts to increase business taxes and regulatory burdens are noticeably silent when it comes to the government failing to support British business in Europe by fostering good relations with our EU partners.

While not all firms would benefit from the UK being part of the eurozone – it is less relevant in some sectors than others – the more that can be done to foster good relations with the EU, the better it will be for a large number of our firms. This is especially true when it comes to being part of the Euro. Maintaining our own currency places a high cost on many companies as well as introducing uncertainty, which is a burden at the best of times, let alone in the current economic situation.

Opponents of British entry to the Euro have taken to insisting that the decision is not economic – presumably they realise they have lost the economic argument – but political. George Osborne is the latest proponent of this fatuous tack.

Yet opposition to the Euro is purely political and expounded by people who tend to be pathologically opposed to Britain having ties with our European neighbours. That is despite this country being deeply entwined with Europe commercially, financially, culturally and socially.

Vision and principle are essential for good government and require an understanding and acceptance of how nations now relate to each other and, from our own point of view, how Britain fits into the global pattern in the 21st century.

Our future cannot be determined by a belief that the UK should slip back to the situation of more than a century ago, when we owned an Empire. The issue is how we as a nation exist in the modern world to the benefit of our people.

David Seymour

Those opposed to the Euro see the pound as a symbol of the might of Great Britain. It certainly is a symbol, but of this country's decreasing influence.

The Euro has become the strongest currency in the world while sterling has slipped close to becoming a basket case, sliding relentlessly.

We used to laugh at the lire, peseta and drachma. There may now be concerns over the economies of Italy, Spain and Greece, but no one laughs at the Euro. Can we still say the same about sterling?

David Seymour - Former Political Editor of the Mirror Group.

Widening the Euro, Deepening Development

Imitation may not, since Rory Bremner and Tina Fey, be quite the sincerest form of flattery. But it's hard to overlook the role of successful Euro transition in reviving interest in currency unions elsewhere. Events have set back the target dates of 2010 for a Gulf Cooperation Council single currency, and 2011 for an Eastern Caribbean States economic union look increasingly ambitious; even more so, the single East Asian currency proposed by the Asian Development Bank's then-president Tadao Chino in 2004, and the African Union's plan for an African Economic Community by 2023. But it's a tribute to the Euro's trouble-free launch, and early

157
Alan Shipman

stability of the Eurozone, that these other currency integrations were suggested and timetabled at all.

The Euro has given emerging economies another, more generally beneficial economic example: one external exchange rate to manage instead of 15. Reductions in exchange risk and transaction cost were a major selling-point of economic and monetary union (EMU) within the EU. These benefits have been proportionally greater for many of its smaller less-developed country (LDC) trading partners.

The Millennium Development Goals are still frustrated by EU foot-dragging on farm reform (disrupting conditions for many low-income agricultural producers); and by its switch to WTO-compliant trade pacts that force reciprocal concessions from those enjoying tariff-free free goods and service trade, with a risk of killing their new industries in infancy. At least, through the Euro, Europe has delivered one important compensation. A single EU currency significantly reduces the costs and risks to LDC central banks of managing exchange rates and external debt with limited reserves - and to LDC businesses of hedging (or gambling with) currency risk when they borrow, exchange capital or engage in trade with Europe.

But the UK's absence from the Eurozone has meant a serious dilution of these emerging-world benefits, especially for countries whose trade was steered towards Britain by colonisation and the subsequent 'sterling area'. It has also weighed heavily on the zone's new members, notably Cyprus and Malta, whose visible tourism trade is still extensively UK-focused but whose imported fuel, goods and services come mainly from Euro-land. Britain's trade integration and structural convergence with other member states, which makes its monetary union with them increasingly appropriate, also means that LDCs once focused on the sterling *or* Euro zones are now deeply engaged with both. These too-frequent victims of 'structural adjustment' await a much less painful policy adjustment, from London, that would lessen the risk of a currency crisis recurring.

Alan Shipman

Raising Capacity, Reducing Complexity

Liberal critics of this reasoning would seek to turn it against itself: arguing that globalisation of trade makes exchange rates irrelevant. Devaluation can, in some cases, subtract via higher import costs as much as it adds in export competitiveness; currency risks can, in principle, be hedged if sufficient financial instruments are available. The consequent irrelevance of exchange rate 'management' could be viewed as precisely the reason most EU states opted into the single currency.

But European monetary union (EMU) was the culmination of many years' real convergence that had made the EU's internal trade mostly intra-industrial, and refocused its external trade on exchange of services (or service-based manufacturing) for raw materials, fossil fuels and commoditised industrial goods. For its structurally different LDC trading partners, measured adjustment of currencies against the Euro remains a vital policy instrument, made easier the fewer large European currencies keep a separate currency floating against the Euro.

Easier exchange-rate and monetary policy conditions are not the only benefit to LDCs of Europe becoming one-currency zone. The larger, more transparent and competitive single market has been made more open to other countries' business. EMU's architects were correct to anticipate its promotion of leaner, less subsidy-hungry enterprises that in some cases could re-substitute imports from lower-cost countries. But removing the veil of multiple currencies also pushed more companies down the US track of outsourcing non-core production and data processing to those countries. The consequently greater flow of capital and technology to states outside the EU has in turn reinforced their trade access, businesses dependent on imported inputs becoming the biggest opponents of 'fortress Europe'.

Cross-Channel Lessons

So long as the UK keeps a separate currency and attempts an independent monetary policy, unpredictable and large sterling:Euro realignments will be an additional - and avoidable - headache for nations that trade with both. If the pound is preserved, more LDC businesses and central bankers will join Eastern Europeans in aligning with the Euro (through target ranges, fixed rates, Euro adoption or euroisation) - and downgrading their trade and investment relations with the UK as they focus on a market more than six times its size.

The UK's indifference towards its former colonies' currency arrangements contrasts with post-war France, which created a currency for the French Community of Africa (CFA) underwritten by its own central bank. France allowed the CFA franc to revalue against the French franc it adjusted this downwards to peg to the US dollar in 1948, and to devalue against the French franc when it pegged this to the prototype Euro in 1994. Twelve African countries stayed with the CFA and switched its parity to the Euro in January 1999, accepting France's case that its entry to a larger currency union would benefit its non-EU trading partners by expanding the market against which they have eliminated currency uncertainty.

On average 50% of African trade is with the EU, but the share is significantly higher for CFA franc countries. There is a strong case that, as a result, France has better insulated its trade advantages from former colonies against erosion by its new EU trade focus. More remarkably, there is a case that France has also bestowed more benefits on its LDC trade partners, in terms of their recent growth rates and income distributions. That's extraordinary when the UK's ex-colonies include such size- and resource-favoured nations as Nigeria, Kenya and South Africa, while Francophone counterparts include the internally war-torn states of Algeria, Rwanda, Congo and Ivory Coast.

Retreat of a Bad Example

The UK's long history of monetary divergence from the rest of Europe – often cited as a reason to stay out of the Eurozone - has generally been bad for itself, other EU states and the emerging world. While Britain's position on most issues may be (as Monnet observed) ten years behind, on development issues it is more usually 35 kilometres adrift - with an unnecessarily enriched *bureau de change* taking the place of the resigned *plus ca change*.

Though its chosen distance from the European project marginalized Britain in most other policy areas, on monetary policy it has often been able to call the European tune, through a transatlantic duet. Most notably, Thatcher's Britain encouraged Reagan's America down the path of financial market deregulation, through a gateway Nixon had forced open by abandoning the dollar exchange standard in 1973 (but couldn't step through before another notorious gate blocked his path).

Removal of capital controls from the early 1980s enabled the UK and US to grow their economies faster by achieving the previously impossible combination of low savings rate and high investment rate. They did so by importing capital from parts of the world where it saving was still in fashion - running far larger current-account deficits than LDCs would have been permitted, not least because the capital those LDCs wished to import found London and New York far more comfortable domiciles than Luanda or New Delhi. But proponents of financial liberalisation also viewed this as a way to help the poorer nations grow faster and close the gap with the richer. Not just through the extra buoyancy of rich-world markets, but because previous capital-market controls were presumed to have left all economies 'financially repressed'.

The liberalisers' main belief - that removing old financial-market barriers would promote investment and growth by raising real interest rates and stimulating saving - always rested on pre-Keynesian theory and has been widely disconfirmed by subsequent experience. Where deregulation has led to faster growth, it is usually by reducing savings and promoting consumption fuelled by credit growth and capital import - unsustainably, as the Anglo-American growth arrest of 2008 painfully showed. But that year's 'credit crunch' also showed how far EU financial institutions, despite their supposedly greater monetary self-containment, had chosen the same path down which to flee 'financial repression'.

It will never be known if bringing the UK into monetary union earlier would have prevented the bubble that has now blown. While deregulation fuelled the supply of easy credit availability that led banks to make loans vastly in excess of their deposits and households to take loans only serviceable through asset appreciation, financial regulation also fuelled the demand for high-yield assets, persuading Continental high-savers to finance the Anglo-American low-saving boom. But this alliance of interests has proved an unholy one. Its implosion has made the prudential policy case - as well as achieving the practical alignment of cycles - required for the UK to distance its central bank geographically from its main financial district, as a matter of urgency.

UK: PLC to LDC

Britain would not only deliver benefits to its developing-country partners by joining the Eurozone; it would avail itself of similar benefits, for much the same reasons. Structurally, the UK shares several LDC attributes. It has run a chronic current-account deficit, mostly with the EU, making it reliant on capital inflow to keep the pound stable; when capital inflows slowed in 2008, the currency fell rapidly. UK households dependent on largely imported food, and businesses dependent on largely imported energy and raw materials, suffer potentially severe cost shocks whenever the currency fluctuates. The increasing numbers of both that have taken out foreign-currency debt are similarly exposed, and largely unable to hedge. Even businesses with available currency hedges are tempted not to use them, as unhedged exposures make windfall profits on the upside.

The gambler's habit is hard to shake off. But, deprived of its ability to draw in capital from the world's external-surplus nations (and struggling to keep alive the banks that had channelled that capital), the UK now has a self-interest in joining a monetary union that its battered wholesale financial institutions and exchanges can no longer be so confident of beating.

A fear among many LDCs, once it became clear that the Delors Plan would succeed where all previous European currency blueprints had failed, was that the Euro area would strengthen its magnetism for foreign investment. Not only the dollar zone, but now also the Euro zone, would reverse the flow of capital from periphery to core, absorbing flight-capital from the less advantaged regions instead of sending more investment their way. But while it has undoubtedly enlarged EU capital markets and made them a safer place to invest, Europe's new monetary bloc has also become a magnet that deflects other flows. There is now a chance of turning the EU-US-Japanese 'triad', already made more rectangular by China, into a genuinely polygonal configuration, adding constructive sides to Europe's 'variable geometry'.

Until the Euro's arrival, only a few late-starting economies - mostly in East Asia and Latin America - had achieved the transplants of capital, technology, enterprise and commercial rules needed to progress from 'emerging' to 'newly industrialising'. In the past ten years other regions, including Africa, South Asia and the non-oil-rich parts of Central Asia, have moved onto the global economic map and into the developing act. Shifts in the EU's role as aid-giver, trading partner and capital exporter have played an important role in this. Unification of its currency and trade policy were key factors in the changed corporate and governmental behaviour promoting these shifts.

The UK, also on the periphery of that unification, now needs inflows of capital and changes of institutional behaviour at least as profound as most emerging economies. By joining, it could capture fuller benefits from Europe's unified market, at the same time as helping spread those benefits beyond the zone.

Alan Shipman – Senior Lecturer, Department of Economics, Open University.

Britain, the Euro and the New Economic Doctrine of the West

To those with a weakness for history, the most striking aspect of the current economic crisis is that it represents the greatest shift of financial power away from the West and towards the East since the fifteenth century. Indeed, some commentators consider we have seen the start of the eventual eclipse of our entire system of free markets interrelated with free societies, and its replacement by the more ordered and collectivist arrangements dictated by so called Asian values. If this were true, the problem is: a world directed on such principles would be a prison.

Free markets in banking and investment have certainly led to the excessive increase, both in the scale and in the complexity of borrowing, and the consequential catastrophic mispricing of credit risk, which has been the immediate cause of the crisis. This was not restrained by regulation, since these free markets have also become international, whereas government remains national. Even the most powerful nation state, the United States, has been proven incapable of predicting the global ramifications of the remedial actions it has attempted, or of preventing them rebounding upon its own citizens.

The more politically aware of these citizens, the middle class, are the principal victims of the crisis. The internationalisation of the economy in recent years has led their salaries to stagnate and rendered their living standards sustainable only by spending funds raised against assets, particularly in housing. Whilst the rapid expansion of debt inflated the price of these, this was sustainable. Now it is not. They, and as the crisis continues to widen, their like in other Western states, consequently no longer feel the free market is working for them. They wish to re-assert the power of government, encapsulated by Barak Obama's victorious slogan: "Yes, we can!". Protectionism, the re-nationalisation of economies, by the bail-out of corporations that are thought systemically, or structurally, or strategically, too important to fail, by competitive devaluations and by outright quotas or tariffs, is already, or could shortly become, ubiquitous. The problem is: contracting wealth creation back down to levels consistent with effective national power, even for the United States, would be tantamount to impoverishment.

However, the failure to do so, even for the United States, is to risk the discrediting of government and thus of democracy. What if the huge hopes now invested in the new President are replaced by the sombre realisation that "No we can't"? Will the retreat from political participation of the past three decades resume, or even accelerate? In Europe the issue is, perhaps, yet more acute. Already, the democratic legitimacy of the European Union, the only mechanism for co-ordinating national policy responses to the crisis so they can be effective, is widely contested. Governments in some Member States, where democracy is only a relatively recent experience, are coming under increasing political pressures as the economic difficulties they face deepen.

Central to such pressures is the fiscal squeeze. Public expenditure across the West, on everything from welfare to warfare, has risen remorselessly in recent years. At the same time, the internationalisation of the economy has also led governments' tax take, relative to growth, to stagnate. Public deficits, both historic and current, have risen to levels which seriously inhibit future productive performance. If the current crisis of the creditworthiness of banks becomes transferred to the creditworthiness of governments which need to borrow in international markets, the severity of the downturn could be seriously exacerbated, along with the political consequences, since the resulting destruction of national wealth would disproportionately impact upon the middle class. The problem is: the stagnation of public revenues, as of household revenues, and the chronic propensity to live beyond our means which this promotes, reflects the increasing difficulty for Western societies of competing with the East.

In short, we must bolster the creditworthiness of governments, contain protectionism and secure the international co-operation, both within the West and then with the East, which will allow a revival of global trade in a context that enhances, rather than diminishes, the competitiveness of our economies, and ensures, in particular, the adequate future regulation of financial services. But this cannot just be a matter of economics. We must also forge a fresh sense of Western solidarity, which will restore the faith, especially of the middle class, in our liberal and individualistic values and of the political institutions designed to give them expression. All an extremely tall order. At the very least, we need a new economic doctrine which is consistent with, and supportive of, these ambitions.

For the current crisis marks the end of the road for the orthodoxy prevailing since the collapse of the Bretton Woods system of fixed exchange rates: that monetary flexibility is the primary mechanism for achieving sustainable growth. It is this economic doctrine, epitomized by Alan Greenspan's now infamous "put": using low interest rates to counteract falls in the stock market, whilst relying on globalisation to restrain inflation, which so fatally supercharged the structural propensity to excess in liberalized financial services. With interest rates presently approaching zero, activist monetary policy is merging into the mere printing of money. Moreover, even such desperate measures can only increase liquidity. They cannot address issues of solvency and may, indeed, raise them for those governments which thereby cause markets to perceive that they are reckless as to the value of their own currencies. There is a danger this is becoming the case for Britain.

Counter cyclical fiscal policy has underpinned monetary policy, especially where the public sector share of total expenditure has been extensive. But with the support of the banking system now breaching all previous peace-time bounds of state intervention, there is a severe risk of public sector financing crowding out private sector investment. Moreover, some governments may be unable to fund such swollen deficits in international capital markets. Running up yet more debt is not obviously the solution to issues of solvency. Indeed, by exciting expectations of further bail-outs in other sectors of their economies, it is, again, likely to cause markets to perceive those governments are reckless of their creditworthiness. In any event, taxpayer support of national employment would be, at best, simply a short-term palliative, unless accompanied by structural strategies to enhance competitivity, which can only be put in place once a medium term perspective on the international economy becomes possible. At worst, it would distort and diminish the general level of trade, upon which Britain is especially dependent.

This is even more true of competitive devaluation, the logical extension of the present aggressive monetary and fiscal activism of Britain and of the United States (though the dollar's reserve status obviously complicates the impact of its exchange rate on international trade). Its supposed advantages were, of course, what caused the break up of the Bretton Woods system. Now, however, with global demand still falling, and likely to remain anaemic for at least the next year, any policy of seeking an export-led recovery, merely through a cheaper currency, is fantasy. Moreover, given the current scale of the increase in money supply, any sustained recovery in global demand, will almost certainly be accompanied by the rapid return of inflation, especially of commodity prices, which a cheaper currency would amplify alarmingly. Slashing the external value of all assets does not obviously alleviate issues of solvency. Indeed, it would seem likely to inhibit international investors from buying the debt of those governments still borrowing from the markets in a currency (their own) over which they retain the right to devalue. There is now a non-negligible risk this applies to Britain.

Surely, surrendering that right offers the best guarantee a government really is resolved to borrow responsibly? Surely, a monetary union is the best foundation for promoting freedom of trade? Surely, surrendering the option of evading the causes of competitive failure through monetary manipulation affords the best prospect that, however difficult, they will instead be tackled effectively? Surely, a monetary union affords the best context for market regulation, especially of financial services? These are essentially, of course, the four key features of the Eurozone: governments become like any other borrowers, the single market is completed by the removal of the exchange rate tariff, supply side deficiencies and other market distortions become transparent and the independent central bank is the key economic institution both for monetary policy and, increasingly, for supervision. Taken together, they constitute a much reinforced version (because clearly a monetary union that abolishes the participating currencies is, by definition, more robust that any system which merely fixes exchange rates) of the economic doctrine of Bretton Woods: that monetary stability is the primary mechanism for achieving sustainable growth.

Britain currently constitutes the most comprehensive demonstration of the failure of the economic doctrine of monetary flexibility. This is the proper background to the issue of our joining the Euro. It is not just that it would make our own path through the recession much easier. That we would not carry the additional burden of having to autonomously re-establish our monetary and fiscal credibility. That we would avoid running the risk both of a sterling and a funding crisis, with all these would imply. That we could sustain our competitive advantage in international financial services, by carrying greater weight in the deliberations to determine their future regulation and, even more, by having a lender of last resort in a global reserve currency. It is that, were we to enter the Eurozone, the chances would be dramatically enhanced of moving Europe and America towards accepting a new orthodoxy of monetary stability, a new Bretton Woods, which provides the best precondition for a proper revival of the economy of the West.

For all Britain's present difficulties, European Monetary Union would be significantly strengthened by our membership. The scale and speed of our recent devaluation, and the resulting distortions of trade now occurring, despite the depressed commercial climate, between, for example, Northern Ireland and the Irish Republic, has already exposed the fallacy that the Single Market can be sustained without all of its participants joining the Euro within a foreseeable timeframe. If we accept this principle, the bedrock of European economic integration will be secured. The situation of, for example, Hungary, or Romania, would become easier. More significant, sterling's adherence would make the Euro as a global reserve currency. It would finally lay to rest those utterly misguided, but nevertheless still pervasive, market perceptions that there is some residual risk the Union could fall apart. This would relieve the immediate pressure on, for example, Greece, or Italy. Above all, it is what will weigh most with the Americans. Given the present protectionist interests in the new Congress, any moves towards formally enhancing trans-Atlantic free trade will be very difficult over the next four years. But an anchoring of the relationship between the Euro and the dollar might well be possible. For once, the old dream of the British Foreign Office, that we are the essential bridge between the European Union and the United States, might have some reality.

Such considerations give the lie to those opponents of Britain entering the Eurozone, who are becoming aware of the momentum building against them and are now seeking to head it off by claiming that our partners would not have us as we do not currently fulfil the Maastricht criteria on deficits and exchange rate volatility, and perhaps more to the point, given the strong ties so many have maintained with American neo-Conservatism, that the United States remains hostile. These normally most assiduous readers of European treaties have failed to understand that the criteria are only for guidance. The decision remains, ultimately, absolutely one for the heads of government of Member States. They have also failed to understand the enormous fluidity of policy, on both sides of the Atlantic, but particularly in Washington, engendered by the economic crisis.

No, the political problems facing our joining the Euro are only in London, or rather, in Westminster. There is no more perfect example, anywhere, of the decadence that has overtaken the Western democratic process and of the sclerosis of the public spirit of the middle class, which is its most proximate cause, than the sorry story of the European issue in Britain. The world's most venerable parliament has failed, for a generation, to face up to the most fundamental question of the nation's future. Politicians, of all parties, have abdicated their cardinal duty in a representative democracy, which is to lead public opinion, in the national interest, preferring instead to follow passively in the wake of the fantasy, ignorance and prejudice provoked and pandered to by narrow media interests. The middle class have been too seduced, and too stressed, by the globalisation of the economy, to care. It did not seem to matter that a stultifying consensus was developing, an inability to think strategically, or critically, an absolute primacy of presentation and of micro-management. The vices which have kept Europe and the Euro off the agenda are the very same that have kept any serious consideration of the structural flaws in our economy off the agenda. But now all the chickens are coming home to roost at once.

It is possible our financial difficulties will be so serious as to force into being the necessary public support for joining the Euro without the intermediary intervention of our reactive and supine supposed representatives in Parliament. But this depends upon the middle class recognizing that the measures which must be taken now are not merely economic, but also political. That what is at stake in this crisis is not just their prosperity, but their liberty. A new orthodoxy of monetary stability can only be a technical element in the necessary moral edifice of an effective international democracy, capable of balancing the international scale of modern commerce. This has always been the key argument for the fullest commitment by Britain to European integration: that our traditions of parliamentary government afforded the best prospect the process, the unique experiment in a multinational rule of law, which the European Union represents, would become anchored in popular engagement. It is now painfully apparent that such a commitment has become necessary to bring about a revival of those traditions here at home too. Not for the first time in our history, in saving ourselves, we could make a critical contribution to saving the West.

John Stevens - Former MEP (1989 to 1999). As Vice Chairman of the European Parliament's Economic & Monetary Affairs Committee, he was specifically responsible for the legislation going through the Parliament for the creation of the Euro.

Sterling and the Myth of UK Economic Performance

Zhou Enlai's celebrated observation, reputedly made in the 1950s, that "It's too early to tell" what impact the French Revolution had had on humanity is a warning to us all. Given all the other choices made over the intervening period, it is difficult enough to assess the consequences of a single policy decision taken in the past, even with the benefit of many years' hindsight. Hence speculating on what life would be like in the UK today if we had permanently locked sterling's exchange rate to those of its major European trading partners in May

173
Nicolas Stevenson

1998 [1] is almost impossible. Needless to say, Mr Gordon Brown knows better, declaring in July 2007 – just days before the onset of the credit crunch that sank Northern Rock, the Republic of Iceland, Lehman Brothers, AIG and much more besides – that the decision not to join the Euro had been "right for Britain and right for Europe".

The aim of this paper is not, therefore, to speculate on how the UK would have fared had the combination of political and economic circumstances been more favourable to Euro membership 10-12 years ago. It is simply to observe how the UK and 10 other founder participants in the single currency actually performed over those 10 years against a number of economic and financial benchmarks. Even on a very cursory reading of the evidence, it becomes apparent that the prevailing wisdom among the UK's policymaking élite, not least Mr Brown – that the "superiority" of the UK's economic performance since 1998 amply justifies the decision not to participate – is based on an extremely partial reading of the data.

To give the "outists" their due, when viewed as a strictly two-horse race, the UK does appear to have "beaten the Euro-zone" on many of our measures over the past 10 years. UK GDP growth averaged 2.5% p.a.; the zone managed 2.1%. UK inflation ran at 1.8% p.a.; the zone averaged 2.1%. UK unemployment was 5.3%; the rate in the zone was 8.6%. Even on the vexed question of the budget balance, the UK deficit "prudently" ran at 1.4% of GDP as against the zone's 1.7%. You can almost see the smile on Mr Brown's face. Britain was clearly "better off out" and the dwindling band of Euro-dreamers should simply have yielded to the powerful logic of economic performance, folded their idealistic tents and moved on.

This, of course, is the myth that the "outists" and their supporters in the press want you to believe. Fact: on almost all of these measures, the UK was consistently out-performed by one or more of the participating members of the monetary union, not just over the whole course, but year by year, with the UK's performance *ranking* slipping steadily against the other participants. If you're happy judging the UK solely against

---

1   I date effective monetary union from May 1998, when the participating currencies' cross-rates were fixed irrevocably and intra-zone devaluations were finally renounced as policy tools. Formal monetary union followed in January 1999 when the Euro superseded the ECU as the EU's official currency and all wholesale financial market transactions moved over to Euro quotation and settlement. Euro notes and coins replaced physical national currencies from January 2002.

a backward-looking average weighed down by Italy and Portugal so be it. But those of us who still believe that the UK's capacity for adaptation and openness to competition give it hefty advantages over less flexible economies have always hoped to see it giving Finland, say, or the Netherlands a run for their money at the top of the performance rankings. As it was, the "standalone" UK – despite its much-vaunted monetary and fiscal policy autonomy – never claimed the lead (except briefly on inflation).

What's worse, from 2005 onward, the UK began slipping behind the Euro-zone average on a number of our measures. Finally, when financial market indicators are taken into account, the verdict is crystal clear. No amount of averaging-over-the-period will generate what looks like a clear "win" for the UK. In the race to minimize the various countries' borrowing costs or maximize the total returns generated by their stock markets, the UK never once got its nose ahead of the Euro-zone average and it finished the 10-year course several lengths behind it in both cases.

The charts below set out the historic record of growth, unemployment, inflation, budget balances, long-term interest rates and common-currency stock-market returns of the UK and the original participants in the Euro[2], both collectively and individually. Without wishing to belittle the current debate about whether such bread-and-butter metrics should give way to some more complex measure of "happiness"(or take account of, say, damage to the environment or social cohesion), it is hoped that readers will accept the political convention that higher output, employment and stock market returns achieved at a lower "cost" in terms of inflation, interest rates and deficits constitute a "good" outcome, towards which all well-meaning governments should be striving.

---

[2]   Output, unemployment, consumer price inflation and budget balance data covering 1998 – 2009e are drawn from Eurostat's *European Economy* series' statistical annexes. The official Euro-zone has obviously expanded to include Greece (2001), Slovenia (2007), Cyprus (2008) and Malta (2008) and is thus not precisely comparable with what I term the €-10, i.e. the original participants less Luxembourg, whose small size results in annual rates of change for certain variables lying well outside ranges that can easily be displayed graphically. For bond yields I have used month-end yields-to-maturity on "benchmark" 10-year government bonds in the UK and the €-10, as recorded by Datastream. There is obviously a risk that slight differences in redemption dates may have distorted the current yields, particularly for comparable credits within the Euro-zone. For stock markets, I have used the broad total return indices favoured by the Federation of European Stock Exchanges (such as the CDAX in Germany and the SBF-250 in France) plus Datastream's broad Euro-zone composite index. Note that these are measures of total returns (i.e. they assume the reinvestment of dividends) and may differ from more popular measures of stock prices (e.g. FTSE100, CAC40, Eurostoxx 50). All returns are measured in Euros (technically in ECUs from January to December 1998).

Nicolas Stevenson

GDP growth, 1998 -2009e

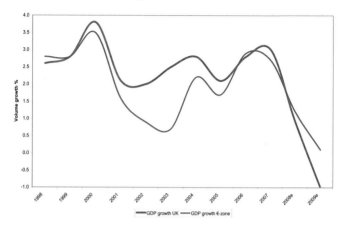

So, let us start with the most popular measure of total economic output, Gross Domestic Product (GDP). Chart 1, or certainly the central part of it, is frequently pressed into service to support what may be termed the Official British View of the rightness of the decision to retain sterling as an independent free-floating currency. UK growth was consistently higher than the Euro zone average from 2000 to 2005. Over the entire 1998 to 2008 period (using Eurostat estimates for the final year), the arithmetic average of UK real, i.e. inflation-adjusted, GDP growth exceeded that of the Euro-zone by around four-tenths of a percentage point per annum. Not having to squeeze the dynamic, globally competitive British economy into the straitjacket of the technically flawed Stability & Growth Pact was clearly of great benefit to the UK, or so we are constantly told. It's a pity about the 2009 outlook, but presumably we can blame that on the credit crunch rather than the independence of sterling…

€-10 and UK: GDP growth, 1998 - 2009e

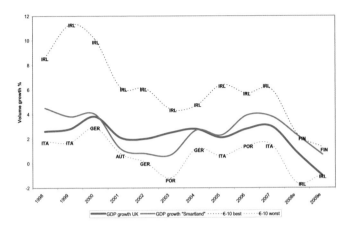

But now look at Chart 2. This plots the annual GDP growth rates of the fastest- and slowest-growing economies in €-10 each year, relative to the UK's performance. As now becomes clear, the UK's actual growth trajectory has broadly followed the middle of the Euro-zone flight-path, between the "over-heaters" (Ireland, Spain) at the top, and the "structurally uncompetitive" (Italy, Portugal) at the bottom. To be scrupulously fair, the UK did grow faster than France and Germany (2.5% p.a. as against 1.8% for the unweighted annual average of the Big Two from 1998 to 2008) but – as was argued at the outset – it is hard to conclude that the superiority of this performance can be ascribed *solely* to non-membership of the Euro and the supposed policy autonomy this brought with it. As the trajectory of our composite 22-million population country, dubbed "Smartland" [3], shows, it *was* possible to deliver marginally superior growth (2.7% p.a.) to that achieved in the UK over the 1998-2008 period from within the Euro-zone, without running into the sort of overheating problems encountered by the higher-growth zone economies or indeed the UK from 2005 onward.

---

3   "Smartland" is a roughly population-weighted (2:1) composite of the Netherlands and Finland. Obviously, the UK could have been painted in an even worse light had I chosen to compare it with "Boomland" (Spain plus Ireland), but I wish to emphasise that it was possible to deliver a performance superior to that of the UK without consistently being the fastest-growing economy in the €-10.

Unemployment rate, 1998 - 2009e

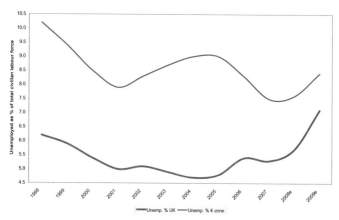

Turning to unemployment (Chart 3), we can see that the standard "UK versus Euro-zone" comparison also favours the "UK knows best" argument. Dynamic, standalone Britain's jobless rate lies consistently below that of the sclerotic Euro-zone over the whole period. Once again, however, it is hard to ascribe this superior performance to the UK's non-membership of the Euro.

€-10 and UK: Unemployment rate, 1998 - 2009e

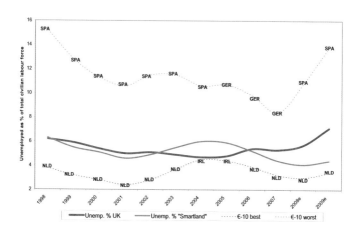

As Chart 4 shows, several Euro participants with open, flexible labour markets delivered lower rates of unemployment than the UK over the period. Ireland, alone of the Euro members, granted unrestricted access to migrant workers from the A8 Central European countries in May 2004, along with the UK and Sweden. Finland followed suit in May 2006 and it went on to trump the UK and Ireland in January 2007 by opening up to Bulgarians and Romanians too. The Netherlands opened its doors to A8 workers in May 2007. As the best/worst chart shows, the UK has lost ground relative to the better Euro-zone performers, as represented by our "Smartland" composite, over the past three years. The most recent Eurostat forecast suggests that the UK will see unemployment over 7% in 2009, its highest level in a dozen years, whereas the zone will see unemployment at 8.5%, well down from the levels of the late 1990s. Naturally, those who claim that the UK has done well by staying out will emphasise the 10-year average and the fact that it still has lower unemployment than the zone. Those who doubt the wisdom of the decision will tend to highlight the UK's worsening relative trend. It's hard to escape the conclusion that satisfactorily functioning labour markets have little or nothing to do with their countries' monetary régimes.

€-10 and UK: Consumer Price inflation, 1998 - 2009e

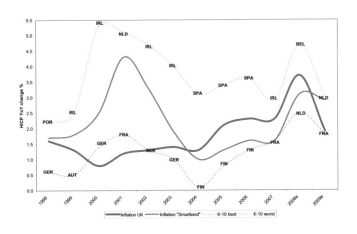

Ironically, the only measure on which the UK was ever "better than the best of the Euro-zone" was inflation: in 2000-04, the UK's 12-month rate of HICP inflation stayed below 1.5%, while the Euro-zone's was over 2%. Back then, there were presumably some members of the pro-sterling lobby who were wary of the Euro on the basis that it was an inherently weak currency and who hoped that the pound would take over from the late lamented Deutsche Mark as the anchor of price stability in the European Union. They aren't particularly vocal today: and no wonder. In 2006, the UK's rate of inflation (2.3%) moved above that of the zone (2.2%) for the first time since 1998. What's more, sensibly managed, steady-growth economies within the zone ("Smartland" again) began delivering rates of inflation around one percentage point below those prevailing in the UK. The undoubted flexibility of the UK's product and labour markets was clearly being offset by something else: a rapidly deteriorating fiscal position, perhaps?

Budget balance, 1998 - 2009e

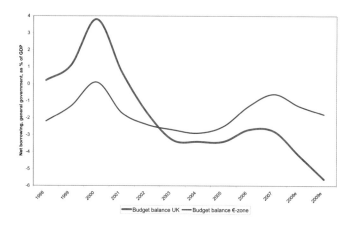

The deterioration of the UK's relative position from 2003 onwards is evident from the "two-horse" budget balance comparison, shown in Chart 6. From 1998-2001, the UK actually ran a general government surplus. As a result, the UK *average* deficit over the entire reference period is still marginally better than that of the Euro-zone. But look at the two trajectories: the proponents of the

Golden Rule at the Treasury (who seriously suggested that only they had "got it" while the tiresome bean-counters in Brussels had failed to understand modern economic management) totally dissipated such fiscal credibility as the standalone UK had amassed in the early years, with the result that the Euro-zone's collective deficit in 2007 – before the onset of the current recession – was more than one percentage point *smaller* than the UK's.

€-10 and UK: Budget balance, 1998 - 2009e

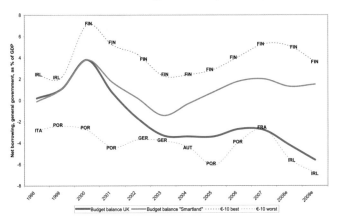

The broader fiscal comparison (Chart 7) shows just how wary we should be of comparing multi-year averages without looking more closely at the underlying data. In 2007 – the year in which it transpires that the US, and probably the global, economy reached its most recent cyclical peak – the UK managed to generate a larger general government deficit than *any* of the €-10. That it is likely to be overtaken on the downward slope by Ireland in 2009-10 is scant compensation for the UK having blown any claim to budgetary prudence outside the Euro-zone. It was cautious, canny Euro-member Finland that went into the recession with a 4% budget surplus, not the famously independent UK. Our "Smartland" composite was also in surplus. To be scrupulously fair, Sweden also managed to brace itself for recession, from outside the Euro-zone, with the help of a 2.3% surplus: but if there were ever an argument for being constrained within the bounds of the Stability & Growth Pact, this surely is it.

€-10 and UK: Benchmark bond yields, 1998 - 2009e

If the deficit numbers alone don't persuade you that the UK outside the Euro is a potentially loose and self-destructive cannon rolling around the European gun-deck, look at what the bond market made of its move away from low inflation and fiscal prudence in 2003-08 (Chart 8). Back in 2000-02, the UK's 10-year sterling gilt yield was often on a par with the very lowest rates payable by the most creditworthy government within the Euro-zone (Germany, at that period and most frequently since). By mid-2005, however, the UK was paying over 50 basis points p.a. more to raise capital in sterling than the *worst* government credit in the Euro-zone (Italy). On this measure, even the old 10-year-trailing-average trick fails to produce a "better" performance for the UK than the average of the zone.

Again being scrupulously fair, in the last few months, spreads within the zone have widened so as to allow the UK's cost of borrowing to sneak in beneath those being paid by Belgium, Italy, Portugal and Spain. But, as was argued earlier, with reference to Euro-zone averages, gaining satisfaction from out-performing structurally challenged economies like Italy or Portugal sells the UK's relatively incorruptible civil service and diligent fiscal authorities woefully short. Why shouldn't the UK borrow on as fine terms as Finland or France, say? Because foreigners don't like holding sterling debt.

On this evidence, issuing debt in Euros – even rather a lot of it – is never going to cost the UK taxpayer as much as financing the comparable deficits in sterling, always assuming that the Euro has, by then, become the currency in which the UK's substantial liabilities (and assets) are denominated. If the supposed benefits of devaluation are only to make themselves felt during the post-recession recovery phase in 2011-13, as now seems to be the "outists'" argument, they will only serve to highlight how unstable the "autonomous" UK economy was allowed to become in the 2005-10 period. Even if this does not prompt domestic policymakers to renounce the potentially instability-inducing weapon of an independent currency (as seems to be happening in Iceland and possibly Denmark and Sweden too), it will certainly contribute to a further widening of the "risk premium" demanded of UK assets by foreigners and possibly prompt calls by them for the UK's devaluation weapon to be "put beyond reach". As others eloquently argue in this collection of papers, concerns over the sustainability of the UK as an international centre for banking and credit – reliant, as it is, on the potentially under-sized home-grown sterling deposit base – make the UK's ability to persuade foreigners that it will pay back their loans a far more important criterion of economic success than the nebulous notion of "export competitiveness", still trumpeted by the pro-(weak-)sterling lobby, in spite of the move from manufacturing to services as the motor of the UK economy.

Equity Markets, Total Returns (€), 1998 -2008 (end-Nov.)

Finally, we come to the most depressing charts of all: the relative performance of the equity markets over the period. It has to be stated at the outset that locally-quoted equities are never perfect proxies for their host economies and that sector composition, takeover rules, savings flows and a host of other factors can affect any given equity market's performance just as much as GDP, inflation, interest rates, relative unit labour costs and what may loosely be termed the "business climate". But it remains an unpalatable fact that the "correct" response by an international fund manager – on hearing of the UK's, or rather Mr Brown's, decision to bottle out of joining the Euro in late-1997, courtesy of the Five Tests – would have been to sell all his UK equities and buy almost anything listed in the then-nascent Euro-zone.

As can be seen from the "two-horse" view (Chart 9), the Euro-zone has returned about 30%, with dividends reinvested, in Euros, over 119 months. Viewed over the same period, the UK market's total return in Euros was negative: it ended November 2008 roughly 7% below where it started in January 1998, at an index level of 93 (Jan 1998 =100). Worse still, the UK never produced higher returns than the Euro-zone composite, so it wasn't even a case of UK equities proving their relative worth during a particular phase of the economic cycle. Admittedly, much of the UK's relative weakness is down to the devaluation of sterling in recent months, but that gives

Nicolas Stevenson

no comfort to international fund managers. They are simply in the business of maximizing their clients' wealth and income in dollars, yen or pesos: but the UK equity market, largely thanks to its host country's unpredictable currency régime, provided a much tougher environment than the comparable Euro-zone markets in which to do so.

€-10 and UK: Equity Markets, Total Returns (€), 1998 -2008 (end-Nov.)

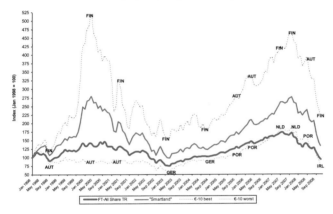

Incredibly, for a sophisticated market that hosts the largest natural resources sector in Europe and where the concept of takeover-proof "national champions" is (rightly) frowned upon, the UK was consistently towards the bottom of the 11-country performance ranking, right from the outset. From mid-2007 to mid-2008, it even managed to underperform the very worst of the €-10 equity markets (at that time Portugal and the Netherlands). To be fair, in recent weeks it has had *la lanterne rouge* snatched from it by Ireland (index level 74), but it is still lagging Germany (103), Italy (114) and France (148) as at end-November 2008.

Doubtless Euro-sceptics will ascribe the Finnish equity market's excellent performance (index level 217) to the presence of world-class technology companies like Nokia, but we suspect that Finland's category-leading position within several of the €-10 rankings (see Charts 2 and 7) won't have done the equity market any harm along the way. We hesitate to wonder just how dynamic the UK market – with equally world-class corporations like BP, Tesco and Vodafone to its credit – would have been if it had enjoyed Finland's supportive economic and business environment these past 10 years. As we remarked at the outset, there were probably many fortuitous policy decisions that have contributed to Finland's enviable 10-year record: but, given the UK's mediocre and deteriorating relative performance, it is now surely up to the "outists" to prove that joining the Euro was not one of them.

Keys to €-10 countries in charts: AUT = Austria, BEL= Belgium, FIN = Finland, FRA = France, GER = Germany, IRL = Ireland (Rep.), ITA = Italy, NLD = Netherlands, POR = Portugal, SPA = Spain.

Nicolas Stevenson - Head of European Equity Strategy at Mirabaud Securities in London. He has worked in European economic and financial analysis for over 30 years.

Facing Reality

One of the many lessons impressed upon us by this extraordinary epoch is that economic and financial developments do not stop at national borders. Anybody who formerly believed that some economies had become decoupled, or that financial market upheavals in the US – or Iceland – would not affect markets in Europe, has been forced to change their minds. More than a year into the crisis, it is a good moment to ask about the consequences for the UK of remaining outside the Euro, and whether the time has come to reconsider that choice.

Part of the answer to this question requires some counterfactual thinking: how would the crisis have unfolded here if the UK had

Peter Sutherland

not so far stayed out? This will shed some light on the cost-benefit calculation made by opponents of the UK's Euro membership prior to its launch in January 1999.

The more interesting discussion looks forward to whether or not it would be better for the UK to seek Euro membership in the near future. What are the implications for interest rates, jobs and incomes, and financial stability of going out or staying in?

The central argument deployed against Britain's membership was always the benefit of an independent monetary policy. The structure of the economy in the UK, and in particular the importance of financial services and the high rate of home ownership financed at variable mortgage rates, meant there would always be an advantage in being able to set interest rates independently. At the time of launch, the ECB's interest rate was half that set by the Bank of England. Opponents of UK membership argued that an immediate interest rate cut on that scale would create a damaging boom in the British economy, a clear demonstration of the unsuitability of one-size-fits-all monetary policy, at least for a distinctively different economy.

With the benefit of hindsight, it is not clear how big an advantage the independent setting of interest rates has been for the UK. The UK's policy rate has remained above the ECB's throughout the period, but with a very similar profile.[1] This pattern looks more like a risk premium on sterling than a genuine divergence in policy.

The housing market doesn't seem to make the UK distinctive either. Its housing boom resembled that in other non-Euro, 'Anglo-Saxon' economies such as the US and Australia, but also the booms in Ireland and the Netherlands, other countries where the ratio of mortgage debt to GDP climbed post-2000.[2] According to recent IMF calculations, the UK is one of the countries which experienced the largest rise in house prices unexplained by fundamentals such as demography and housing supply, but so too are Ireland, France and Spain.[3] Some commentators have argued that over-stimulating the housing boom was a consequence of joining the Euro for Ireland

---

1 Except for a period in 2004.
2 IMF World Economic Outlook April 2008, Chapter 3.
3 IMF World Economic Outlook, October 2008, p17.

and Spain. However, this argument is flawed. The Netherlands had a boom too despite joining the single currency without a big interest rate cut in 1999, while staying out did not preserve the UK from its housing bubble.[4] A wider range of factors than interest rate policy alone, including debt levels and the structure of mortgage finance, seems to explain differences between countries in their recent housing market experience.

As for the UK's relative dependence on finance, the share of GDP accounted for by the output of financial services was somewhat higher in the UK than in the Eurozone, but not dramatically so.[5] In this respect the distinctiveness of the British economy looks to have been exaggerated. The key difference is that a greater proportion of the output of the UK's financial services industry is exported.

One aspect of flexibility the UK has clearly enjoyed during the crisis looks like a mixed blessing, namely the scope for a devaluation. The pound has fallen to successive record lows against the Euro (it has lost more than a tenth of its value against the Euro and fallen by nearly 18% against a basket of major currencies this year). At the time of writing, parity seemed to beckon in the not too distant future, and with it the danger of an old-fashioned sterling crisis.

As an immediate mechanism for responding to a severe shock to the economy, the scope to adjust by devaluation might be very welcome. Yet anybody who recalls the UK's dismal post-war history of recurrent devaluations after a period of excessive boom, all too often laying the foundations for a subsequent inflationary episode and the pattern of boom and bust, will be depressed by this echo of the past failures of monetary policy.[6] Depreciation will help the balance of payments adjust but like any other means of adjustment it imposes a loss of purchasing power on British people. A reduction in income is the only means by which a persistent current account deficit can be closed, but the devaluation route is the one with the most unpredictable distributional effects. Moreover, as the recent

---

4   See for example Martin Wolf, *Why eurozone membership is still no answer for Britain*, Financial Times, 19 November 2008.
5   The figures are UK about 8%, Eurozone 6.5%.
6   The main albeit striking exception to the pattern of post-devaluation inflations was after the UK's sudden exit from the ERM in 1992, when new monetary arrangements and the favourable productivity shocks of the mid-1990s prevented the subsequent from being inflationary.

example of Spain demonstrates, a balance of payments deficit can be reduced within the Eurozone by a considered fiscal adjustment.[7] It is only in the UK that the devaluation option is seen as an attractive alternative in the circumstances of financial crisis. In Denmark, Sweden and central European countries, the context of financial and currency market turbulence is seen as a strong argument for Euro membership. The verdict of the currency markets at present is that the British economy now looks more like Iceland's than like the Eurozone's, hardly a good verdict on our monetary independence.

The weakness of the pound is of course temporarily very helpful to British exporters (although not importers), but exchange rate volatility is not a favourable pattern for companies trading with our main market. Last year the Eurozone accounted for 31% of UK goods and services exports and 35% of UK imports.[8] Price volatility on the scale we have seen is extreme, and difficult for businesses trading inside the Eurozone to manage, especially those building their sales on high quality products and strong supply chain relationships. Currency volatility undermines efforts to build long-term supply relationships.

This takes us to the heart of the long-term economic case for Britain's membership of the Euro. The single currency completed the single market by removing a significant piece of grit in the cogs of trade. There is a growing amount of research confirming that the Euro has modestly boosted trade between members.[9] Firms in member countries are more likely than before to export within the Euro area, and are trading more products than they used to. The effects are larger for smaller firms.[10] The Nobel Laureate Paul Krugman predicted before the launch of the Euro that there would be a restructuring of Eurozone industries, with a smaller number of larger clusters in particular industries, drawing on supply chains

---

7   In the year to September 2008, Spain's imports grew by 4%, its exports by 16%.
8   ONS figures, compares with 35% and 41% for UK's total EU exports and imports, and 9% and 6% for the UK's US exports and imports. The Eurozone accounts for 51% of exports of goods, and 48% of goods imports.
9   See for example Richard Baldwin, 'The Euro's Trade Effects' ECB Working Paper No. 594, March 2006. Andrew Rose, 'One Money, One Market' Economic Policy 2000, 30:9-45 found a much larger effect, but the consensus is that the trade boost has been modest and occurred in the early stages after the launch of the currency. See Gianluca Cafiso, ECB Working Paper 941 September 2008, 'The Euro's Influence on Trade', for a recent summary; it concludes that the reduction in transactions costs in the EZ did not affect trade, but the removal of uncertainty, and increased price transparency did boost trade.
10   See a summary survey of the empirical research at http://voxeu.org/index.php?q=node/26

190
Peter Sutherland

within the Eurozone. In other words, the single currency would remove exchange rate uncertainty and transactions costs, and over time enable European industry to catch up with the economies of scale and efficiencies demonstrated by US industries. There is indirect evidence that this process has occurred in the convergence of prices within the Eurozone, to a point where it now resembles the level of price dispersion in the US.[11]

This process has been most marked in sectors where there has been a substantial re-organisation of supply chains in the Eurozone, under the pressure of competition in the single market. The car industry is a good example. Price differences have narrowed throughout the EU15, but more so in the Eurozone countries, with exchange rate variation between the Euro and the 'outs' providing the scope for less convergence in the latter case.[12] While the UK remains an important producer and exporter of vehicles and certain components, there has been a reorganisation of the supply chain by the main Eurozone producers. The impending recession will be painful for all of Europe's auto industry; we might find it is more acute for the UK's producers and suppliers.

For the UK is not only outside the Euro, but also geographically peripheral. The UK is now a smaller trader than the main Eurozone economies: in 2007, our total exports accounted for 16% of GDP, compared with 21% for France, 24% for Italy and 42% for Germany.[13]

The pre-1999 debate about the Euro was marred by exaggeration. It was not an instant disaster for Britain that the pound stayed out. If output and trade in some industries are now lower than they might otherwise have been, the differences still are small – although they will cumulate to large shortfalls over time.

---

11   A number of studies have documented price convergence, including market research by AC Nielsen http://nl.nielsen.com/site/documents/breakingnews_europe.pdf, econometric research eg John H Rogers, Monetary union, price level convergence, and inflation: How close is Europe to the USA?, Institute for International Economics 2006, and research conducted for HM Treasury's assessment of the 'five tests' http://www.hm-treasury.gov.uk/d/adessex03_exec_92.pdf

12   'Price Convergence in the European Car Market' Salvador Gil-Pareja and Simón Sosvilla-Rivero, *Applied Economics*, 2008. vol. 40(2), pages 241-250.

13   Eurostat figures.

Peter Sutherland

It will not do to over-claim for membership of the Euro now, even though the UK's economic circumstances are precarious in the extreme. No doubt there will be serious economic strains within the Eurozone. Yet there are several reasons why the case for UK membership of the single currency should be reconsidered urgently.

- It is absolutely timely to safeguard the pound. The currency markets may not have reached the limits of their evaluation of the financial robustness of the UK, with its large-scale dependence on capital imports to finance balance of payments deficits. The last time the UK had a balance of payments surplus was (for one quarter only) 1998, and by mid-2008 the deficit had reached 3% of GDP. By definition, a current account deficit has to be matched by a capital account surplus, or inflows of foreign capital. Investment into the UK cannot be sustained at these levels. The balance of payments deficits will have to decline, and there are only two mechanisms for this – a recession which reduces imports and a fall in the pound. We will get both, but there is a serious risk of a full-scale sterling crisis.

- Even looking beyond the short-term fallout from the financial crisis, an independent sterling is likely over the longer term to be a rather weak currency on the periphery of the Euro, which will increasingly be used as a reserve currency alongside the dollar. The risk premium in UK interest rates which already seems to have been present since the launch of the Euro will remain and probably be bigger in the foreseeable future. Higher real interest rates will weigh on business and individual borrowers in the UK, and on taxpayers who will ultimately be paying the interest on the massive increase in government debt.

- The shape of post-crisis financial regulation is unclear but will certainly need to be more closely co-ordinated than in the past. Banking regulation at the level of the Eurozone has already become somewhat more politically acceptable. Although it is hard to know what the full implications of non-membership of the Euro in terms of financial regulation will be for the UK, it is certain that Britain's peripheral voice in shaping that architecture would be weak.

- In Britain we face the particular challenge of assessing the contribution of the City to the wider economy, and restoring its strong position in international markets, in a sustainable manner. A return to highly liberal and lightly regulated markets, characterised by massive financial innovation and much offshore activity, is not on the cards. Given the impact of the credit crunch on the intellectual climate, that might not happen for another decade or even a generation. It is unlikely that the City of London will fare as well outside the Euro in an era of stricter regulation as it did in an era of deregulation.

Gordon Brown and Alistair Darling have put much weight on the need for international co-ordination of the monetary and fiscal policy response to the crisis. And rightly so. We have learned the hard way through the course of 2008 that the interlinked global economy fares better with co-ordinated policies. The same logic applies to the even more closely linked EU economies, and recognition of this fact means there is likely to be better co-ordination of fiscal policy in the Eurozone in future. Outside the Euro, the UK will be outside that process and will not be shaping the rules. The UK's current leadership in discussions of the international economic and financial architecture will prove ephemeral if the country insists on remaining outside the most relevant part of the framework of co-ordination for its own economy.

Peter Sutherland – Former EU Commissioner. Now Chairman of BP plc.

Britain and the Euro

Until the credit crunch and the onset of recession (or worse), entry of the UK into the Eurozone was a taboo subject not mentioned in polite society. Today it is hard to see how it can be avoided in any serious discussion of the future of sterling or the City or Britain's role in Europe.

The arguments have changed. Some of the fears expressed in 1997 by pro-Europeans about the effects of a failure to adopt the Euro have proved unfounded, at least in the last ten years. We have not had higher inflation than other EU members. Foreign direct investment did not dry up. Because of a variety of international crises, we did not lose all influence in the councils

195
Dick Taverne

of the EU. And despite our exclusion from the Eurozone, the City has flourished.

The problems we now face are different: a crisis of stability and credibility and the danger of deflation. To avoid heavy unemployment we need Keynesian policies of low interest rates and more government borrowing. We need public spending and tax cuts. However sterling, for long a strong and stable currency, has recently become very vulnerable to speculation, its weakness aggravated by our level of personal indebtedness (53 per cent of the total EU credit card debt in the European Union). More large-scale government borrowing can only increase the risk of further devaluation. If the pound suffers a serious collapse, it will cause the mother and father of economic crises, which would force us to raise, not cut, interest rates and cut, not increase, public spending in order to restore international confidence. We would have to do the opposite of what is needed to avoid depression and heavy unemployment.

Though sterling is a small reserve currency, amounting to only some 4 or 5 per cent of the reserve currencies of the world, this role still adds to its vulnerability. If those who hold sterling fear a collapse, they will quickly switch to Euros or dollars, adding to downward pressure. How much more secure and stable our economy would be if we were comfortably ensconced in the Eurozone and if our trade and our overseas investments and liabilities were backed by the Euro, one of the world's two major reserve currencies, much safer and more stable than the pound.

This brings me to the second argument, that about the future of the City. There is a widespread, smug assumption that the role of the City as a world financial centre is secure and that its present pre-eminent status will safely survive the upheavals in the world's financial systems. It is taken for granted that the traumatic experience of a tiny country like Iceland has no relevance to a much larger, well-established economy such as that of the UK.

But why did Iceland's banks collapse? Not because they were insolvent or because the country's economy was badly managed, but because the banks, like many others elsewhere, were overwhelmed by the unexpected liquidity crisis in wholesale financial markets. Iceland is a very small country with a large financial sector, huge in relation to its GDP. It is internationally active and internationally exposed. International exposure did not prove fatal to most banks in other countries, however much they suffered, because most were bailed out by their governments. It proved fatal to Iceland's banks and to its economy because Iceland has its own currency.

All banks can be regarded as risky businesses, because they borrow short and lend or invest long. If all their depositors suddenly want their money back, they cannot pay even if they are fundamentally solvent with long term assets normally exceeding their short term liabilities. In the case of domestic banks, a country's central bank can act as a lender of last resort to tide them over, since it has the security of the value of their long-term assets. It can rescue perfectly sound domestic banks if there is a crisis of liquidity. If necessary, it can print more money.

However, a central bank can only act as saviour if it can lend in the currency in which liabilities have to be met. It cannot print foreign money. Iceland's banks borrowed and invested abroad in foreign currencies and incurred foreign liabilities on a massive scale, amounting to about eight times Iceland's GDP. Its central bank could not act as a lender of last resort in foreign currencies. The story would have been different if Iceland had been a part of the Eurozone. After all, the case of Iceland was not unique. Ireland might well have gone the way of Iceland if Ireland had retained its own currency and had **not** been part of the Eurozone.

Any suggestion that the UK can be compared with Iceland has been met with ridicule and, of course, the UK is much larger and has more international credibility. However, there are some highly relevant similarities.

Financial services also form an important part of our economy. Our financial institutions, too, have borrowed and lent or invested in foreign currencies on a massive scale, amounting to well over four times our GDP. That compares with a figure of some 100 per cent of GDP in the United States and some 30 per cent in the Eurozone. The Bank of England is also unable to act as lender or market maker of last resort if UK banks cannot roll over their short-term liabilities denominated in foreign currency or if they cannot sell their foreign currency assets because of a shortage of liquidity in wholesale markets. Of course the Bank of England can arrange swaps and credit lines with other central banks, but only at a considerable cost. And what would happen if the Bank of England lost credibility because of a collapse of sterling?

As Willem Buiter has argued, the UK is placed somewhere in the middle between Iceland and the reserve-currency countries, ie. the United States and the Eurozone. Indeed in some ways we are closer to Iceland, because sterling is not a major global currency and we are very minor players on the global scene. And even if the Bank of England or the financial institutions themselves can provide insurance against demands to meet their liabilities in foreign currencies, the cost of such insurance would place the City of London at a competitive disadvantage, which it may not easily be able to afford.

Admittedly the arguments for joining the Eurozone are not all one way. The ability to set our own interest rates can be useful. But as the experience of Australia and New Zealand has shown, this advantage can be overrated and will count for little in a crisis. The Bank of England has also told us that interest rates are not a suitable instrument to prevent an asset bubble, one of the main causes of the present crisis.

It should also be conceded that if we had joined the Eurozone at the start with a greatly over-valued exchange rate, we would have had to make the kind of adjustment Germany had to make. This might have benefited productivity, but would have been a painful experience. Today the problem is rather the reverse: how willing would France be, for example, to accept us as a Eurozone member at our present exchange rate, which now gives us such a competitive advantage?

There is one final argument for joining the Euro that has largely been neglected. As mentioned, we did not lose as much influence as I had expected by staying out in 1997. But circumstances are now very different. Other countries, notably Denmark and Sweden, thought like Britain that they should preserve their economic independence by keeping their own currencies and controlling their own interest rates. Polls suggest they have now changed their minds. Most recently joined members of the EU also want to join the Eurozone. It is very likely, if we keep the pound, that we will be virtually the only EU member left outside. It will not be glorious isolation. We will have no say in the vital discussions about any new European regulatory regime. We will be more outside the mainstream of the EU than we have been since we first became part of the Union. Our influence in the world as well as our economy will suffer.

Dick Taverne - Former Labour MP and Financial Secretary to the Treasury who resigned from the Labour Party over its opposition to entry into the European Community in 1972 and was re-elected as an independent social democrat in 1973. In 1979 he was a member of the Spierenburg Committee looking at the reform of the European Commission. He now sits as a Liberal Democrat in the House of Lords.

The UK Framework for Macroeconomic Policy

Ever since the exit of sterling from the Exchange Rate Mechanism in September 1992 the UK government has argued that the incentives for considering participation in Economic and Monetary Union (EMU) were decisively weakened by the development of a superior framework for macroeconomic policy in the United Kingdom. Quite apart from the political considerations in the UK public debate weighing against any such participation and the so-called "five tests" formulated in 1997 by the incoming Labour government to be met before entry into EMU could be considered, confidence in the monetary and fiscal framework developed in London has

Niels Thygesen

played a major role in dismissing EMU from the political agenda. But recent events strongly suggest that any idea of superiority in economic management relative to the rest of the European Union has become untenable. Even though the recent focus in the UK debate has – quite understandably - been on the deteriorating fiscal outlook, it may be appropriate to start this brief comment with the UK monetary framework which was developed first and with some considerable success.

Inflation targeting, Central Bank independence and the sterling exchange rate

Very quickly after the abolition of the commitment to keep sterling within the ERM-band the Bank of England moved – along with Sweden and following the promising examples of New Zealand and Canada – to adopt inflation targeting. This policy had clearly positive effects, even before the Bank was given operational independence in 1997 to achieve the inflation target set by the government. The new status was accompanied by better transparency in policy-making, facilitated by the structure of the decision-making body, the Monetary Policy Committee. A more explicit and symmetric inflation target than practiced elsewhere in Europe and – more significantly – a good record in keeping the inflation rate within the band prescribed helped to lift confidence in the monetary framework and encourage self-congratulations relative to efforts elsewhere. For about a decade UK monetary policy seemed well-designed to play a major role in macroeconomic stabilization, not only of inflation, but more generally.

Over the past year the confidence based on past achievements has gradually been eroded. The inflation rate rose and the Governor of the Bank had to write twice to the Chancellor to explain the reasons why it had transgressed the band. The reasons could initially be ascribed to external inflationary factors, but domestic inflation was also picking up, a housing boom underpinned by large household indebtedness had built up and begun to deflate, while the trade and current account deficits were widening. Rising interest rates to dampen domestic inflation had tended in the short term to strengthen sterling, providing an additional reason for external deficits. More recently interest rates have been cut drastically to mitigate the downswing in the UK as in other economies as the consequences of the financial turmoil spread to the real economy, and sterling depreciated rapidly in effective rate terms. Given recent forecasts for the UK economy with negative growth in 2009 and a slightly falling price level, further interest rate cuts are to be expected on the basis of the mandate for monetary policy - with further depreciation of sterling appearing inevitable.

It is well recognized that monetary policy can not target inflation and the exchange rate at the same time. But the other side of the coin of successful achievement of the UK inflation target for a long time is that the exchange rate of sterling has gone through major cycles. There have been two main examples since 1992: the strength of sterling around 2000 and again up to 2007. The former of these episodes made important parts of the UK manufacturing sector uncompetitive – and the consolation that this was not serious, since services, and particularly financial services, were now becoming more important and highly competitive has proved to be short-lived. The second period of sterling strength which is currently being (more than) undone may have helped to combat inflation, but has aggravated the downturn in the economy. So the evaluation of the monetary framework must be more mixed than it appeared one or two years ago : while technically competent, the focus on inflation targeting has permitted swings in the exchange rate which have taken on such an amplitude that they now have to attract the attention of policy makers. Having an independent monetary policy may be an asset for an economy of the size of the United Kingdom, but if the imbalances in the current and in the public sector accounts become serious, conflicts between external and domestic considerations are hard to avoid. To assess whether that is currently the case for the United Kingdom requires a critical look at the fiscal policy framework.

An alternative fiscal framework for the United Kingdom?

When the Labour government came into power in 1997 much emphasis was put on a strengthening of the framework for fiscal policy, designed to combine macroeconomic stabilization with longer-term sustainability of public finances. Two provisions were introduced to assure this combination: the golden rule and the sustainable investment rule. The former committed the UK government to a policy of borrowing only to invest and not to fund current spending over the economic cycle. The latter set the level of public debt relative to national income to be kept under 40 per cent. Both of these rules seemed very sensible at the time of their introduction, but developments over the past couple of years have made it clear that they can not be maintained. Indeed, they have both been suspended in the recent Pre-Budget Report, published by the Treasury on 24 November 2008. In the following the reasons for this suspension are reviewed from the special perspective of determining whether this step could bring the United Kingdom closer to following the fiscal framework of the Stability and Growth Pact (SGP) which underpins EMU. Over the past decade UK officials have often emphasized the appropriateness of the provisions of their framework as more flexible and intelligent than the allegedly more arbitrary and primitive practice followed – and sometimes not followed – on the Continent. But the differences have narrowed and, as the UK framework has been suspended, the SGP has become more flexible and "Intelligent". There is now every reason for the United Kingdom to reconsider its attitude of superiority regarding the SGP.

The golden rule exempted public investment from the requirement of a cumulative balance (or small surplus) over the cycle because there had been a tendency over a couple of decades to try to consolidate public finances by disproportionally postponing investment. The need for improving the public capital stock in the health, education and transport sectors was generally recognized. While this objective could have been assured in other ways, it was felt that the distinction between investment and consumption was sufficiently unambiguous to make monitoring possible. The fiscal rules in EMU considered the same choice initially, partly because a golden rule had been

Niels Thygesen

part of budgetary practice in Germany throughout the post-war period, but it was decided to focus on the balance including public investment, largely to avoid the risk of creative accounting. With the heavy investments undertaken in the United Kingdom over the past decade, a special status for capital expenditures may no longer seem essential; projected expenditures in the above-mentioned areas suggest that the surge is not to continue, so that this particular difference from the practice in EMU can no longer be regarded as essential to preserve.

A more important difference is the way in which the concept of "balance over the cycle" is measured. It has attracted unfavorable attention that the UK Treasury could determine the dating of the cycle over which balance was to be observed. By extending the initial cycle backwards from 1999 by two years into a period with surpluses the Treasury was able to claim, when the cycle ended in 2006, that a small surplus of a little more than 1 per cent of national income had been achieved cumulatively over the entire cycle. But this backward-looking dating implied that the next cycle was starting with a deficit, raising the risk that fiscal policy would have to be tightened in a pro-cyclical way at some point – a risk that would now have materialized, if the golden rule had still been in operation. The essence of the Pre-Budget message is not that some stimulus is being set in motion, notably by the temporary cut in VAT, but that the starting point for the public finances has worsened so much; revenue corresponding to 4 per cent of national income appears to have been permanently lost, raising the current deficit for 2009-10 to 5.3% and the total public sector borrowing requirement to 8% of national income in that year.

In these circumstances the Pre-Budget document wisely abandons any reference to balancing the budget over a cycle that has become impossible to date. It refers instead to a pure forward-looking rule prescribing a declining path for the cyclically-adjusted current deficit "as the economy emerges from the downturn". This is rather similar terminology to that used by the EU Council of Ministers when it formulates budgetary guidelines on the proposals of the Commission. Even the pace at which the Chancellor foresees consolidation to proceed from 2010-11 is similar to the minimum

205
Niels Thygesen

of 0.5% used in the SGP. The main difference with practice under the latter is that a government with as unfavorable a starting point as that of the UK would be under stronger pressure to speed up its back-loaded consolidation.

The UK government, when it introduced its fiscal rules more than a decade ago, raised the justifiable criticism of the original version of the SGP (also agreed in 1997) that it was excessively focused on the budgetary balance in a single year – "a snap-shot photo" – and not enough on underlying trends. This initial deficiency, prompted by fear that the underlying, or cyclically-adjusted, balance would be too hard to monitor, has now been overcome, and the SGP (as revised in 2005) relies in its preventive arm on a forward-looking measure of the cyclically-adjusted balance. The United Kingdom, as a member of the EU, is also subject to the SGP, but the rules are given less prominence in countries not participating in EMU - and particularly in the United Kingdom where budgetary documents seem to be solely prepared for domestic consumption, using national frameworks and definitions (which remain a bit different from those used by the Commission). Given the convergence in practice that has nevertheless occurred between the UK fiscal framework and that of the SGP, it would seem logical for the UK government to adopt the latter now that superiority for the former can no longer be claimed.

The second part of the original UK framework – the upper limit to the public debt ratio – offers an important additional argument in favor of such a step. At the end of 2006, nearly a decade after the rule was introduced, the debt ratio stood at 36 per cent, apparently comfortably below the limit – which was already a good deal lower than the limits observed by the main EMU-participants, Germany and France, not to speak of Italy. With the erosion of UK public finances occurring at a faster pace than on the Continent, the UK debt ratio a few years hence will look rather similar to those of the other main countries in Europe. In order to direct focus more on this – unfortunate – convergence rather than on the worsening of the UK position in isolation, more open allegiance to the SGP framework could be helpful.

There is, of course, one important remaining difference between the UK economy and those of the EMU members. The UK government has to fund its rapidly growing public debt in its own currency, and the pressures on the monetary authorities to keep very low interest rates to stabilize the domestic economy do not make it easier to attract funding without further undesirable slides in the sterling exchange rate. Also for this reason it may be desirable for the UK authorities to appear more as a part of a European policy space than as an individual economy even more affected by the international downturn than its European neighbours.

Niels Thygesen – Former member of the Delors Committee on EMU (1988 to 1989). Now Emeritus Professor of Economics, University of Copenhagen.

Don't Mention the Euro

"The only thing we have to fear is fear itself" said President Roosevelt. He could have been talking about the timidity of pro-European British politicians. In fact, he could have been talking about the inhibitions most mainstream politicians have about expressing any point of view that steps outside the prevailing, Daily Mail-led consensus.

In this essay, I shall be examining the forces that have caused politicians to become followers rather than leaders. Why do they lack the courage of their convictions? What can be done to stiffen their backbones?

209
Simon Titley

At the time of writing, British membership of the Euro is moving back onto the political agenda. But it is telling that this is happening less because of any principled argument, more as a panic-fuelled reaction to the economic crisis in general and the slide in the value of sterling in particular. Some pro-euro commentators are coming out of hiding, but their tone remains apologetic.

Roy Denman, in his book 'Missed Chances', and Hugo Young in 'This Blessed Plot', catalogued Britain's sorry post-war history of imperial hubris and lost opportunities. Those of us who have supported Britain's membership of the common currency have seen the failure to join as another of these missed chances. But we should beware of rubbing our hands with glee at the thought that the economic crisis will make membership inevitable. If these are the circumstances in which Britain joins the Euro, the currency will remain the object of simmering resentment, perceived as a symbol of national humiliation. Crisis or not, it is vital that supporters of the Euro make a principled and upbeat case, and argue for Britain to join on the most advantageous terms.

Why the timidity and the apologetic tone, the recourse to expediency instead of principled advocacy? To understand, we need to go back to the revolutionary social changes of the 1960s and 1970s, which led to the replacement of tribal politics with individualised consumer politics. Before this era, most people had their identities given to them by the traditional groups to which they belonged: family, geographical community, social class or church. Today, most people create their own identities and select their own peer groups. We make ourselves. This individualism was brought about by a combination of affluence, education, secularisation, technological advance and sexual liberation, which released the majority of people from lives circumscribed by day-to-day subsistence and group dogma, and popularised the concept of 'lifestyle choice'.

As people began to cast off their traditional social identities and search for something new, consumerism filled the void. People reoriented their identities around the things they buy. One can see this transformation in the way products are advertised. Previously, products would be advertised according to functional benefits such as price or durability. Nowadays, advertising has moved from rational considerations to emotional appeals about how a product makes one feel about oneself.

People also began to apply consumerist expectations to politics. Instead of seeing their interests shared with those of a traditional group, they developed an expectation that politicians could provide a bespoke offer. The trouble is, unlike the marketer of a consumer product, able to target a niche market, politicians are simply unable to satisfy millions of individualised wants simultaneously. Voters perceive this inability as impotence or dishonesty, and a vicious cycle of disillusionment and alienation sets in.

It was not until the 1990s that most politicians began to realise what was happening. They responded by adopting a consumerist strategy, moving from leadership to followership, from ideological positioning towards consumer appeal. This trend was reinforced by the alleged 'end of ideology', when it was claimed that all the big questions had been settled; and globalisation, which limited politicians' freedom of manoeuvre and capacity to deliver. Ideology has not ended, but the range of ideas has narrowed considerably, politics has been replaced by managerialism, and the argument within the political mainstream is confined to a debate about nuances or replaced by personality issues.

The disappearance of profound ideological differences in the 1990s was accompanied by the importation from the US of election campaign techniques modelled on the psychoanalytical methods developed in advertising and marketing, in particular the use of focus groups. These electoral techniques replaced an ideological approach with a consumerist one, characterised by emotional appeals to the self. For example, Focus groups were highly influential on New Labour. Former spin-doctor Derek Draper once joked, 'A bunch of eight people sipping wine in Kettering determined pretty much everything Labour did'.

The result is that politicians, instead of engaging in ideological argument with one another, now compete to agree with public opinion. They no longer have any incentive to support a cause unless it can already demonstrate public support. Hence the torrent of ill-considered 'initiatives' generated in response to each tabloid-led episode of moral panic.

If the identification of public opinion is the Holy Grail for politicians, what are politicians recognising as 'public opinion'? It is generally perceived as the opinion with the highest profile and the strongest emotional force. And this is where the pro-European cause has come unstuck, because it has failed to adjust to the new political culture. When the 1975 referendum on Britain remaining in Europe was won, pro-Europeans regarded it as 'mission accomplished'. In retrospect, the enthusiasm and passionate argument of the referendum campaign should have been maintained to establish firmer foundations. Instead, the field was left clear for anti-Europeans to dominate and frame the debate. The national press is overwhelmingly hostile to the EU, while the letters pages of local papers throughout the country are filled with ill-informed rants by UKIP supporters. Nowhere can one find the equivalent drive and passion from pro-Europeans.

But the pro-European cause is far from lost. The bi-annual 'Eurobarometer' opinion poll, commissioned by the European Commission, shows fairly consistent levels of support for the EU. Roughly speaking, one-third of the British people supports the EU; one-third opposes it; while the remaining third has no strong opinions either way. The fact that supporters at least equal opponents in number is remarkable considering the deluge of anti-European propaganda that has poured out of Britain's right-wing press for more than thirty years, and the absence of an effective pro-European campaign since the 1975 referendum. It is no cause for complacency but it is certainly no reason for pro-Europeans to hoist the white flag.

Furthermore, the 'Eurobarometer' poll indicates that pro-Europeans tend to be younger and better educated than Eurosceptics, suggesting that the pro-European cause can benefit from a growing and more articulate segment of opinion, if anyone bothered to mobilise it.

Simon Titley

Taking all this into account, the prerequisite for a successful campaign for Britain to join the Euro is moral courage. This is difficult for politicians who are used to pandering to what they perceive as majority opinion. But the paradox of politicians attempting to locate and appease a 'middle ground' of popular opinion is that it actually turns people off because it makes politicians seem indistinguishable from one another.

Politics is ultimately about making moral choices. Standing up for one's beliefs provides people with a choice. Indeed, a revival of real politics is not possible without fighting a battle of ideas over competing visions of how to organise society. It would be healthier for all politicians to be clear what they stand for and to fight for coherent positions with integrity. It is a myth that people don't like political arguments. Argument is what differentiates parties and provides people with a real choice. What people actually don't like is when politicians look and sound the same. So-called 'voter apathy' is a rational response by voters unable to distinguish between what is on offer.

An overriding desire to seek a consensus also hobbles politicians with a fear of causing offence. They would be much better off being true to themselves and not trying to please everyone. The pro-Euro lobby should accept that its beliefs are deeply unpopular in some quarters. One cannot attract without also repelling. There is more to gain by building support among those who share its values than by trying to appease those who don't.

There is no point having a policy unless one is prepared to argue for it passionately. Pro-Euro politicians and other opinion-leaders should not sit and wait for the collapse of sterling or assume the inevitable. They must offer some moral leadership, to provide a rallying point for like-minded people and help change the terms of the debate. Until now, Eurosceptics have been free to frame the debate in Britain because they are the only ones expressing clear and consistent values, however wrong they may be.

Further, the pro-Euro argument must marry the rational to the emotional. There is a strong rational case for joining the Euro, which still needs to be argued. But that must be complemented by an emotional appeal that reaches hearts as well as minds. Theodore Zeldin, writing in the Observer (29 May 2005) following the French 'no' vote in the constitutional referendum, remarked:

"Europe is a fact. But it still needs to become a dream. ...the French [referendum] campaign has shown that the European constitution, written by lawyers focusing on rules and regulations, rather than by poets expressing new emotions, allows old emotions to prevail."

If the economic crisis proves particularly bad for Britain, winning the argument for joining the Euro could be achieved by default. Might it not be better to win the argument by providing not just dry statistics but also a dream of how much better a post-crisis Britain could become as a member of the Eurozone?

Simon Titley - Former Liberal parliamentary candidate. Now a writer and public affairs consultant based in Brussels. Member of the Editorial board for the Journal of Political Marketing and co-editor of the magazine "Liberator".

Joining the Euro: Not Just Britain's Place in Europe, but Europe's in the World

In the spring of 2003, the Chancellor of the Exchequer, Gordon Brown, advised Prime Minister Tony Blair that the five tests for British membership of the Eurozone had not been met. At the same time, a very senior Treasury official told me that, while there would probably never be ideal convergence between the British and Eurozone economies, there was sufficient convergence for British membership to take place. It was, he said, now more a political decision than an economic one.

It was pretty apparent that Gordon Brown had taken a political decision. Cabinet ministers were shown the eighteen detailed analyses which fed into the final assessment and were subsequently shown the assessment. A number of them commented that the conclusions in the assessment were more negative than the findings in the detailed studies. And they saw the assessment only *after* Tony Blair had spent weeks arguing with Gordon Brown to change the tone, if not the substance, of the conclusions.

At the time, the whole drama was as much a microcosm of the debilitating struggle between Blair and Brown, which dogged Tony Blair's ten years as Prime Minister, as an argument about policy priorities. It was, according to Labour insiders, a reversal of the position each man had taken in Opposition, when Tony Blair had been more cautious than Gordon Brown in his support for British membership of the Euro. Yet, I believed at the time that Tony Blair's commitment to taking Britain into the Euro in Labour's second term was genuine. The economics had to be right. Not only did Britain's economy have to be competitively flexible to cope with the straitjacket of centrally fixed interest and exchange rates, but the economies of our partners had to be more flexible too. But Blair believed, or so I believed, that there was a strong political and economic case around the trade-boosting effects of membership, the risk of losing inward investment and the loss of influence we would suffer over the strategic direction of European economic policy if we stayed outside.

Those views were shared, in a pretty broad-brush way, by a majority of the Cabinet. They wanted the direction of travel to be toward Euro membership. Above all, though, they wanted the Prime Minister and Chancellor to stop quarrelling, and to be seen by the public to stop quarrelling. And, in the end, Tony Blair wanted, not so much to convince Gordon Brown that the time had come to recommend membership and to call a referendum as to make it clear, without expressing it precisely in terms, that the issue was not *whether* to join but *when* to join. In that, he failed and, with scarcely a backward glance, both Blair and Brown consigned British membership of the Euro to the dustbin of discarded Labour policies.

A referendum without the Prime Minister and Chancellor on the same side of the argument would have been un-winnable and Gordon Brown can certainly be criticised for helping, by his behaviour, to turn that truth into a self-fulfilling prophecy. But the increasing unpopularity of the Iraq conflict would probably have made a referendum on the Euro un-winnable in any event. Meanwhile, the British economy outperformed many of its continental partners. The Eurozone countries did not move to fiscal harmonisation or to a more coherent and exclusive economic governance that would have been damaging to Britain as an outsider. Gordon Brown was seen to have been right. The Euro became a non issue.

Five years later, the British economic story looks more like bubble than model. There is at least a reasoned fear that our gross (in the moral sense) indebtedness will make our economy more vulnerable than that of many of our key partners. The desirable flexibility of a floating exchange rate may not look quite so attractive in the long term. The Eurozone may start to loom as a safe haven in the stormy darkness.

I doubt that it alone would be enough to tempt the British people to vote for Euro membership. Memories of our enforced withdrawal from the Exchange Rate Mechanism may now be dimming but the perception remains strong that we hitched our wagon to a European star, fell to earth with a bump but picked ourselves up and were stronger on our own. The inconvenient truth that, but for ERM membership, we would not have lowered inflation and broken the long cycle of stop go economics that had bedevilled us since World War II is now forgotten. What sticks is the strong sense of: once bitten, twice shy.

You can argue a similar counter-factual case in respect of the financial melt down. Just as it was only ERM membership that enabled us to beat inflation, so membership of the Eurozone from 2002 might have created the impetus for a happy medium between our light touch regulation, which turns out to have been perilously hands-off, and the more centralising and regulatory instincts of our partners. As it is, we went our way and, in the perception of many, put a poison pill into the system.

It is also arguable that British membership of the Eurozone would have made it possible for the European Union to take some of the political steps envisaged in the original concept of economic and monetary union but not so far attempted. Most British politicians, and a majority of the public, would argue that the only circumstances in which British member ship of the Euro could be contemplated at all would be in the *absence* of anything approaching a political union. If a British government ever wanted to put the case in a referendum it would have to argue that the fears entertained by Margaret Thatcher in the late 1990s, that economic union would only work as part of political union and that such a political union represented an unacceptable degradation of national sovereignty, had proved groundless. Yet it is the absence of political will, and therefore of political integration, which constrains the EU governments from taking the steps towards closer coordination of economic and fiscal policy which are necessary if European countries are to remain competitive.

We Europeans have huge advantages. Together, we account for 30% of the world's GDP; we are the biggest concentration of stable democracies; through our aid and trade relationships with the rest of the world we exercise influence. We are the epitome of the successful exercise of soft power. The future is too unpredictable to say with confidence that this will be the Asian century. In particular, the impact of climate change could be both devastating as a natural disaster and the cause of as yet unforeseen conflicts. Nor do we know whether the Chinese model of prosperity without democracy will prove sustainable. What is sure, however, is that we will be part of a multi polar world and there is no single European country that can, by itself, constitute one of those poles. Only Europe united, politically and economically, can do so. And that is impossible while we run our economic and fiscal policies on the present national bases.

During much of my lifetime, until the advent of Margaret Thatcher, we tolerated our national economic decline. It was sufficiently slow and genteel to be bearable. Maybe the same will be true of Europe as a whole. That will certainly be our fate if we do not take dramatic action, action that has to reinvigorate the process of European integration so that we have genuinely common economic, fiscal, energy and foreign policies.

For that to happen Britain will have to be part of the Eurozone.

Many will dismiss this as airy-fairy idealism. Which was exactly what de Gaulle said of the Schumann Plan, the brainchild of Jean Monnet, and the foundation of the Coal and Steel Community which was the basis of Europe's post-war unity and prosperity. If we continue to think small we should not be surprised to find our prosperity and influence equally and painfully diminished.

Stephen Wall – Formerly Britain's Permanent Representative to the EU (1995-2000) and Tony Blair's EU adviser in Downing Street (2000-2004). His account of British EU policy under Prime Ministers Thatcher, Major and Blair (A Stranger in Europe) was published in 2008.

The Curse of the House of Atreus

To date, nobody has actually served up a fricassee of their nephews and nieces as the prime delicacies in a feast for their brother. Nonetheless, Britain's relationship with its continental neighbours has all the ingredients of a curse in a Greek Tragedy which entails the sins of the fathers being endlessly repeated from generation to generation.

Fifty-three years ago, the British made their first major miscalculation at the Messina Conference which led to the founding of the European Community. The Government sent a delegate, but withdrew him long before the Six worked out the details of the Treaty of Rome. The delegate had predicted that the nations present would not agree. Even if they did, he claimed, it would not happen. Even if it did happen, it would not work. The European cause had few political adherents at the time. Harold Macmillan himself, later a genuine Europhile, was lukewarm about the prospect. For the Labour opposition, Herbert Morrison predicted that, should Britain participate, it would be "the end of Britain as an independent European state" and "the end of a thousand years of history." At least his family broke with the traditions of the House of Atreus with his Europhile grandson Peter Mandelson.

As Dean Acheson said a few years afterwards, Britain had lost an Empire and failed to find a role. Participation in the European project at the outset would have given the British a strong role. Instead, we preferred to look backwards to a position in the world which we were bound to lose, rejecting in 1955 the anti-nationalism of our fellow Europeans and then, in a strangely parallel miscalculation the following year, the supposed nationalist threat of Gamal Abdul Nasser. Had we abandoned the illusion that we were still a major imperial power and participated in the Community at the outset, we could have shaped the rules to suit us far better, notably on agriculture. We were then forced to try and reverse the mistake against the hostility of General de Gaulle, eventually joining sixteen years later than the founder members and on far less favourable terms than we would have had at the beginning.

Inevitably, Britain was regarded, even after our entry, as a semi-detached member of the club. Indeed, there was a serious attempt to pull us out again in 1975. When the Referendum was first mooted, public opinion was in favour of withdrawal by around two to one, the ratio turning round almost exactly by polling day because of the strengths of the pro-European cross-party alliance and the weaknesses of the antis.

The surge of pro-European sentiment was short-lived. By the early 1980s, Margaret Thatcher was fighting an abrasive battle to get "our money" back. By the end of the decade Brussels had replaced the Argentines and Arthur Scargill as public enemy number one. Britain, she said, had not successfully rolled back the frontiers of the state only to see them reimposed at European level, with a European superstate exercising a new dominance from Brussels. Cheered on by a little Englander press, the Government found it much easier to tilt at largely fictional European Aunt Sallies than to explain the real reasons for its failings.

Pro-Europeans like Roy Jenkins despaired of the tunnel vision on display. He wrote in 1985, "If we are confident of our future up until and beyond the year 2000, we must get our head out of the groceries and retain the vision, nerve and perspective of those who more than thirty years ago were responsible for the European Community's creation."

Perhaps the most eloquent description of Britain's failure of vision came in the famous resignation speech of Sir Geoffrey Howe in 1990. "The Prime Minister's perceived attitude towards Europe is running increasingly serious risks for the future of our nation. It risks minimising our influence and maximising our chances of being once again shut out. We have paid heavily in the past for late starts and squandered opportunities in Europe. We dare not let that happen again. If we detach ourselves completely, as a party or a nation, from the middle ground of Europe, the effects will be incalculable and very hard ever to correct."

Sadly, however, opportunities continued to be squandered, starts stayed persistently late and heads remained consistently stuck in the groceries. Britain still looked half-hearted members of the club. We signed up to Maastricht, but opted out of preparations for the Euro, the Schengen Agreement and the Social Chapter.

In 1997, the chance finally came to bury the curse of the House of Atreus. "Under my leadership", said the new Prime Minister Tony Blair, "I will never allow this country to be isolated or left behind in Europe." After his astonishing landslide victory, Blair could have done anything he wanted. Here, apparently, was a Prime Minister who could actually speak French quite well and was committed to the European cause.

This was a moment for leadership, and sadly the leadership was found wanting. It would be unfair to underestimate the forces which were mobilised to stop Tony Blair taking Britain into the Euro. The press, overwhelmingly pro-European at the time of the 1975 Referendum, was now, with a few exceptions, stridently anti-European. As a result, public opinion was against entry. Remembering the party's four successive General Election defeats, New Labour was terrified of losing the public support which it had only recently acquired. There were also, of course, forces within the Government opposed to entry, most formidably the Chancellor Gordon Brown, whose press spokesman Charlie Wheelan helped to torpedo the project with his famous mobile phone call from the Red Lion pub in Westminster. The mood music in much of the commentariat uncannily echoed the British position at Messina. The Euro wouldn't happen. If it did happen, it wouldn't work.

Despite all this, Tony Blair could have taken Britain into the Euro, if not at its formation at least within a couple of years. His own prestige was higher than that of any of his adversaries. He could have won a Referendum. Admittedly, the starting position was public opposition to the Euro. It was not, however, a very salient concern. Voters were much more interested in jobs, schools and healthcare. Most admitted that they did not know enough about the issue. Had a strong campaign been mounted, public opinion could have been turned round, just as it was in 1975.

Instead, the issue was ducked. Britain was saddled with higher interest rates, less inward investment and far greater vulnerability to pressures from the world economy. Politically, our loss was even greater. The Prime Minister who had promised never to be isolated or left behind was treated with exactly the same suspicion as his predecessors by his European allies. He drifted more and more into the orbit of President George W. Bush, with whom he launched one of the most ill-judged wars in British history. Tony Blair had become yet another victim of the curse of the House of Atreus.

Over the years since its launch, the economic case for the Euro has looked stronger at some times than others. The political case has always been overwhelming. Both Britain and the EU would be stronger if we played a full, unambiguous role in Europe, and we can never do that while we remain outside the eurozone.

The downturn in the world economy has unleashed some very powerful forces. It is just possible that, amidst all the other destruction which they cause, they might finally blast away the curse of the House of Atreus from the British Government. History will stop repeating itself and we can at last resume the role in Europe which we should have been playing ever since the Second World War.

David Walter - Former Political Correspondent for ITN, Channel Four News and the BBC, former BBC Paris Correspondent and Presenter of the Radio 4 programme Europhile. Former Director of Communications for the Liberal Democrats and parliamentary candidate, now an independent writer, broadcaster and media strategist.

The Battle for Public Opinion: Learning from Past Mistakes

Following the successful ratification of the Single European Act and Jacques Delors' launch of the process that would eventually see the establishment of the Euro, it was widely believed that, set backs notwithstanding, the "ever closer union" envisaged in the Treaty of Rome was an inevitable historical process. As far as the United Kingdom was concerned, a series of events, the Bruges speech in September 1988, the fall of Margaret Thatcher, the tortured negotiations that produced the Maastricht Treaty, the Danish No and the coruscating and deeply divisive debate over ratification, unleashed sceptical forces in Britain succeeded in turning these assumptions upside down.

Michael Welsh

Although there was never a serious movement to withdraw from the EU altogether, the belief that some of the powers ceded to Brussels could and should be clawed back rapidly gained ground; whether or not Britain should join the Euro became the fulcrum of the national debate. Action Centre for Europe sponsored an enquiry chaired by former Governor of the Bank of England, Lord Kingsdown, his report was an erudite statement of the economic case for Britain joining. Business for Sterling rallied the City against the Euro with an aggressive and well-funded public relations campaign. The public, bemused by the jargon, quickly became bored, not least because of the uncompromising terms in which the argument was conducted; joining the Euro quickly became a surrogate for being pro or anti Europe, an argument in which reason was submerged in emotional rhetoric. By the time Labour came to power in 1997 there was a settled view that the British people would never agree to surrender the pound, accordingly there was no point in trying to persuade them to do so. When Britain in Europe was launched the following spring, supposedly to prepare for a referendum, the public argument had been irretrievably lost.

Nothing is set in concrete: in three generations sentiment in Britain has moved from anti to pro Europe and now back to anti again. Each tectonic shift breeds an over-reaction that in turn produces a correction. Who is to say that in the coming period there will not be another revolution in the public perception of Britain's European role? It is possible to envisage conditions in which the Government of the day might conclude that joining the single currency was in the national interest. The question is whether it would be able to carry the consequent referendum in the face of engrained Euro-scepticism and a viscerally hostile media.

In the 1990s the pro–Euro argument focused on the economic and political advantages which might accrue from joining the Euro if it came into being; for the most part the debate was conducted by economists, academics and other experts in terms that left the ordinary person cold. While joining is the immediate issue and therefore a key component in any debate, it must be understood that it derives from a much larger question – the nature and extent of Britain's engagement in the European project. If the case is made for the European Union the case for the Euro will follow; the converse doesn't work. The failure to address the nub of the question – do we wish to be part of the European Union or not? – presented the sceptics with an open goal; they could trump the economic argument by asserting that it was all a dastardly plot to undermine Britain's sovereign independence.

This problem was exacerbated by the elitist nature of the pro-European case. The perception that European Union is a *trahison de clercs*, a conspiracy whereby an unwelcome regime is forced on ordinary people by a self-interested governing class has become deeply entrenched. Matters have not been helped by the shift in public attitudes to political leaders: whereas Roy Jenkins, the epitome of an establishment figure, was a positive asset in 1975, the sight of Michael Heseltine, Kenneth Clarke and Charles Kennedy sharing the IMAX stage with Tony Blair and Gordon Brown at the launch of Britain in Europe in May 1998 tended to confirm the impression that dirty work was afoot.

Business for Sterling was quick to exploit this weakness, they deliberately did not use the great and good to put their message across. Instead their spokesmen tended to be anonymous businessmen backed up with plenty of comment from columnists in the tabloid press. They were able to position themselves as standing up for the ordinary man who was not going to be patronised by an overweening establishment.

By contrast Britain in Europe treated the whole affair as a public relations exercise dominated by the No 10 press office. Their exclusive audience was a limited pool of journalists and commentators who were courted with briefings and special events on the grounds that they could be relied on to relay a positive message. It was a classic New Labour approach that didn't work because the Government, riven by faction, was never clear about its own objectives. Downing Street, which kept Britain in Europe on a tight rein, was more concerned with not rocking the boat than rallying support; as a result the considerable latent support for the Euro was never mobilised.

These errors were compounded by a tendency to re-fight the last campaign, in this case the successful referendum of 1975. Paid regional organisers were expected to form voluntary committees without any clear idea of the message they were supposed to be getting across. Volunteers proved hard to recruit, meetings were poorly attended and it became clear that this traditional approach to grass roots campaigning was out of tune with the times. Tensions quickly emerged between the centre and the regional organisers, who were discouraged from taking any local initiatives. There were high profile campaign launches featuring local personalities but no follow up: cynicism and demoralisation quickly set in.

If the United Kingdom is to join the Euro area at some time in the future, the Government of the day must be unequivocally committed to the policy on the grounds that it reflects Britain's national interest and this must be supported by a national consensus that, as Margaret Thatcher put it: *"Britain's destiny is in Europe as part of the Community."*[1]

Initiatives such as the Sutherland Report will play their part in winning the technical argument and persuading the Government to adopt the policy but a very different kind of effort will be necessary to change public opinion. This will involve building public enthusiasm for the concept of a European Union of independent sovereign states by demonstrating that it offers solutions to the intractable problems of the global economy and a way out of the difficulties and uncertainties which face all European democracies.

The manifest inability of nation states to act independently under conditions of failing financial markets, recession, unemployment and falling living standards provides a context in which this kind of movement becomes possible though not perhaps in the short term. Much will depend on the ability of the EU's leaders to rise to the occasion and re-establish the credibility of collective action through the European Union as the solution to our problems. Ever since Harold Macmillan launched the first British application to join the EEC, politicians and commentators have been defensive about Britain's European vocation: at best it has been seen as a shelter to

---

1   Bruges, September 20 1988

Michael Welsh

be grudgingly accepted for fear of something worse or more often as a relentless threat to Britain's national identity which can only be averted through constant vigilance on the part of our leaders.

This mindset can only be changed by a concerted act of will at all levels of political society. Those of us who count ourselves pro-Europeans must start airing our views in public, in private and round the breakfast table. The blogosphere offers opportunities for mass communication, not dreamed of in the 1990s; the European Movement should study the techniques used by Barrack Obama's campaign team to reach millions of voters previously untouched by the political process and see how they could be adapted to British conditions. The Commission and the European Parliament should invest in user-friendly web sites with well presented information calculated to attract the casual surfer. Public-spirited sponsors who support think tanks and other public policy bodies should increase their support for those putting out a pro-European message and businesses large and small who routinely interact and trade with Europe should be encouraged to talk up these aspects of their activities underlining its importance for jobs and prosperity.

Throughout its history the European Union has allowed itself to appear remote from ordinary people and too difficult for any but experts to understand, a misperception encouraged by governments of all political stripes, anxious to talk up their national credentials. If Britain is ever to join the Euro, public enthusiasm for the European ideal must be re-established and, drawing on the lessons of the past, those who truly believe that this is the way ahead must set about making it happen.

Michael Welsh - Former MEP (1979-1994). Former Chief Executive, Action Centre for Europe (1994-2000). Now Leader of Lancashire County Council.

The Lost Decade:
New Labour and Euro Membership

Back on the agenda

The UK has now been outside the Euro for a decade. This has been to the cost of British influence within the EU by placing the UK outside the most important component of European integration. The failure to develop a clear national plan and a timetable for membership is the most striking failure of the European policy of the New Labour government during its period in office.

233
Richard Whitman

The New Labour government is now being forced, reluctantly, respond to an emerging public debate on UK membership of the Euro. However, this does present problems for the Gordon Brown-led administration as it has sought to remove the issue of Euro membership from the political agenda over the last decade rather than to lead a public debate in support of joining the Eurozone.

The current financial crisis has seen a re-emergence of voices in labour movement and at the grass roots of the Labour Party asking whether it might be time for a rethink on joining the Eurozone. This debate has not been generated from within New Labour itself but rather been fuelled by external intervention such as the French radio interview in early December in which Commission President José Manuel Barroso asserted that UK membership was "closer than ever before". Barroso's assertion forced the Prime Minister Gordon Brown to respond publicly that no change in the current New Labour position.

The prompt intervention by Gordon Brown was an attempt to quash a Euro-membership debate in the UK – and by extension the Party and the Labour movement - and to maintain the existing policy of the British Government: that Euro entry is a goal, but one for an indeterminate future date and when 'conditions apply'.

The lost decade

The Blair-Brown administrations have not challenged the fundamental tenet of John Major's government in securing an indefinite opt-out for the UK of the currency union aspects of Economic and Monetary Union (EMU) as a part of Major's price for agreement to the Maastricht Treaty in December 1991. New Labour was thus a bystander at the creation of the Eurozone on 1st January 1999.

New Labour has also not sought to alter the opt-out arrangement on the single currency (despite ending it opt out on the social chapter). Neither has it sought to advance a policy of joining the ERM II since the events of 'Black Wednesday' in September 1992. Although New Labour has stated a formal commitment to Eurozone entry, this is with the important proviso that entry should be endorsed by the public through a referendum following Parliamentary approval. As the referendum requirement is also the policy of both the Conservative and Liberal Democrat Parties, the government policy is essentially indistinguishable from that of the opposition parties.

There was a great deal of speculation during the first term of Tony Blair's government about when a referendum would be held. Blair did not exercise decisive leadership by seeking to swing New Labour behind a timetable for membership. And in 1997 then Chancellor of the Exchequer Gordon Brown and his advisor Ed Balls removed this from the realm of New Labour policy debate by devising five economic tests that would be used as the basis of assessment as to whether the UK was in a position to seek Euro entry or not. This policy stance has not generated any significant opposition with the Parliamentary Labour Party nor the Trade Union movement. Consequently, heading the UK Treasury as Chancellor, Gordon Brown's responsibility for overseeing the assessments as whether the UK meets these tests (conducted in October 1997 and June 2003) has been undertaken without the need to consider an organised constituency within the Labour Party pressing for a favourable assessment. It is therefore unsurprising that these assessments reached the same conclusion in ruling out membership as the conditions for entry were not met in full. The absence of any reassessment since the 2005 General Election has not been the cause of any concern within the Labour Party.

Prospects for membership

Tony Blair's government's European policy can best be characterised as one which stabilised the UK's relationship with the EU and its member states. The UK became a more 'normal' member of the EU by generally seeking more consensus with other member states than the conflict that had been apparent during the Thatcher and Major administrations. However, as Blair did not seriously pursue the prospect of Euro membership, Britain has largely remained outside the 'hard core' of the integration process and New Labour cannot make a great claim to have effected a profound shift in Britain's position within the EU. Gordon Brown's European policy has not departed significantly from Blair's. The differences have been those of style and emphasis rather than of policy substance on the Euro. The Brown cabinet's two most enthusiastic pro-Europeans Foreign Secretary David Miliband and the former EU Commissioner Lord Mandelson has not sought to force a reconsideration of policy on the Euro.

Why might New Labour seek a shift of policy on the Euro now? The financial crisis and attendant recession has resulted in significant job losses in both the manufacturing and financial services. The Trade Union movement is seeing a significant impact on its membership base across these two sectors and providing the rationale for a rethink on Euro membership, driven by an emphasis on the stability and security that membership of a larger currency union and the monetary policy of the European Central Bank might provide. This argument would gather further momentum if the Eurozone appears to weathering the financial crisis and the attendant global recession significantly better than the UK. However, there are also additional factors that may drive New Labour to consider a change of policy.

Electoral politics will be the most important factor in any move to Euro membership by the UK. At present public opinion still remains hostile and winning a referendum on Eurozone entry presents a formidable obstacle to any UK government. The EU is, however, an issue on which there are substantial policy differences between the Labour and Conservative parties. The Tories have set themselves squarely against any further integration through the European Union and have committed to rescind the Lisbon Treaty (the successor to the ill-fated Constitutional Treaty): a policy stance which would throw the UK's relationship with other EU member states into crisis. This policy divide on the EU would allow Brown to claim that the Tory stance is driven more by ideology than pragmatism. Furthermore, for Gordon Brown to bring the UK into the Euro would represent a leadership achievement that was beyond Tony

Blair and confound the critics of his European policy in the UK and in the other EU member states. Eurozone membership is highly unlikely to be the *primary* platform on which the Brown government seeks re-election although the labour movement may seek a strengthening of the commitment to membership in the party's general election manifesto.

Richard Whitman – Former Head of the European Programme at Chatham House. Now Professor of Politics at the University of Bath.

A Hypothetical History:
Had Britain Entered the EMU

Suppose that Britain had entered the Euro when it was founded at the beginning of 1999, instead of spending ten years inventing reasons as to why entry would be a bad idea. It is commonly assumed that this would have been a terrible mistake, and that loss of the exchange-rate instrument would have imposed a catastrophic cost on the economy. The intent of this paper is to examine this contention.

I do not intend for one moment to disparage the importance of having a roughly right exchange rate for achieving sensible

239

John Williamson

macroeconomic outcomes. Far from it: my argument is that Britain would have had an exchange rate consistently closer to its real needs if it had been in the Euro than it had with an independently floating pound. Of course, that depends upon the entry rate being roughly right and the real rate not being carried somewhere greatly different, e.g. by differential inflation. Both of these conditions were in my view likely to have been satisfied. It also requires the condition that there be no important shock that would have required a substantially different real rate.

The Entry Rate

It is common knowledge that Britain could not have entered the Euro at a rate greatly different from one the Bundesbank regarded as sound. One could not enter at a rate so undervalued that the Bundesbank feared it would give rise to an inflationary impulse in the Euro area or threaten Germany's trading interest, nor at a rate so overvalued that the Bundesbank expected to be presented with bailout bills. It is true that German officials commonly mouthed at G-7 meetings the same sort of platitudes as most of their peers, about the impossibility of making sensible judgements about whether or not currencies were close to their fair value. But the Bundesbank acted far more intelligently than German officials spoke: look, for example, at its opposition to the overvalued rate at which Nigel Lawson had put the pound in the ERM in 1989, and its consequential refusal to rescue the pound in 1992. Discomfort at the depths the pound plummeted to after 1992 doubtless made the Bundesbank unhappy too, though there is no public record of its misgivings comparable to the one that emerged after the ERM crisis.

What rate would have been picked if the pound had been a candidate to enter the Euro at the start of 1999? The actual market rate was about 1.45, which happens to be close to the mean for the period[1]. This is a rate well within the limits of historical experience (Figure 1). There is no reason to imagine that it is the sort of entry rate that would have been blocked as unrealistic by the Bundesbank.

---

1   A recent exercise conducted at our Institute and published earlier this year in a Policy Brief by William R. Cline and myself entitled *New Estimates of Fundamental Equilibrium Exchange Rates* gave a somewhat weaker estimate of the FEER-equivalent rate of 1.3 euros per pound. Doubtless there are those who would have argued for a rate of 1.5, but 1.3 to 1.5 pretty much straddles the range of plausible estimates.

John Williamson

Euro-pound nominal and real exchange rates
January 1990 to October 2008

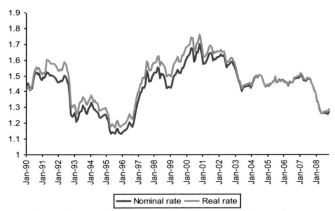

Sources: The Bank of England, the European Central Bank and the UK National Statics Online
Note: The nominal rate for the Euro was proxied by that for the DM prior to 1999

Changes in Equilibrium Exchange Rates

Even if a currency enters a currency union at a competitive but not
inflation-inducing rate, the rate will become inappropriate over time
if the equilibrium rate changes. The most important source of such
changes in the past has unquestionably been differential inflation. At
one time many Latin American countries devalued regularly to avoid
losing competitiveness, and in the days of rapid British inflation
many of us thought that Britain should have followed their example.
Is there a threat that Britain could have become overvalued within
the Euro because British inflation exceeded that of our neighbours?

This question can be answered pretty definitively by comparing
actual inflation rates in Britain and in the Euro area, as is done in
Fig. 2. It can be observed that aggregate Euro area inflation was
somewhat greater than that in Britain: the days of Britain as one
of Europe's chronic inflaters are (mercifully) over. As can be seen,
inflation in Italy has been a lot more severe, and has served to erode
Italian competitiveness to a point where there is discussion about
whether Italy may one day be forced to withdraw from the Euro.
Reversing that loss of competitiveness without a devaluation is
going to be painful, but will be essential if Italy is to remain part of

241
John Williamson

the Euro area. It is clearly desirable that Britain never face this type of situation if it did become part of the Euro area. But the import of Fig.2 is clear: unless performance deteriorates notably in the future, there is no reason to fear such an outcome.

**CPI levels for the Euro Area and the United Kingdom -
January 1999 to October 2008
(index 1999 = 100)**

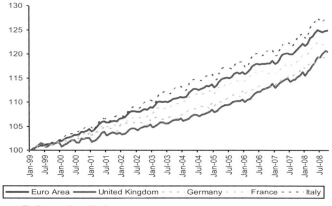

Sources: The European Central Bank

There are several other possible reasons for equilibrium exchange rates to change over time. Productivity may grow more or less rapidly than in competitive countries, with fast-growing countries tending to appreciate (the Balassa-Samuelson effect). However, one of the advantages of forming a currency union with other countries at a similar stage of development is that there is a negligible chance of such an effect proving embarrassingly large. (The East European countries are another matter: this may well constitute a serious difficulty for several of them even before they enter the Euro.)

Another reason that equilibrium exchange rates might change is through accumulation of foreign assets. If a country ran large surpluses on current account, the interest income that it could expect to get on the assets it was accumulating would make it progressively less necessary to have a competitive exchange rate to generate the exports needed to earn the foreign exchange to pay for imports.

However, except for countries in which oil exports are large relative to the size of the national economy, the changes from accumulation or decumulation of foreign assets are going to be slow, ensuring that it will be possible to make offsetting changes through differential inflation.

These are the three sources for most changes in equilibrium exchange rates. One can never rule out the possibility that Britain is going to make some new discovery that will transform its balance of payments prospects independently of them, but it is not sensible to block change on account of the remote possibility that some unforeseen event will occur. All three sources give one confidence that Britain could live with a fixed nominal exchange rate against the Euro area. There will continue to be a need for modest changes in the real exchange rate, but these can be achieved by changes in differential inflation, which is no longer a loose cannon threatening to lead the real exchange rate astray.

Real Shocks that Needed Neutralizing

Those who believe that Britain was better off with a floating pound presumably believe that it floated up in 1997 and 1999 and down in 2002 and 2007 to neutralize some shocks to the economy. If one buys the argument in the preceding section, that neither differential inflation nor differential productivity growth nor foreign asset accumulation created a big change in the equilibrium exchange rate, presumably they think there was some other real shock to the economy. They should specify what shock this was and what useful social function was performed by having the pound first float up and then down, presumptively imposing all sorts of real adjustments that served no obvious social purpose.

It seems clear that the real reason that the pound moved was that financial fads changed. In the 2000s it became fashionable to channel big flows of funds to countries like Britain and the United States that were prepared to run big current account deficits. It is precisely to defend the country against being held hostage to such financial fads that one wishes to see the pound's real exchange rate fixed at an equilibrium level in terms of our major trading partner.

The History that Might Have Been

Look again at Figure 1. The rate at which it is reasonable to assume that the pound would have joined the Euro, 1.3 to 1.5, is within the range in which the Euro-pound rate in fact moved. At the time of formation of the Euro, and for a number of years thereafter, the pound was stronger than its hypothesized entry rate. And recently it has reverted (as after its expulsion from the ERM) to a rate even weaker than 1.3.

Received wisdom argues that it was a good thing that the pound was free to float up in the early years of the period and to float down later on. Had this not been so, the UK would have been faced with inflation in the early years, inflation which it would have been impossible to counteract because monetary policy would have been run by the European Central Bank rather than by the Bank of England and directed toward British needs. In contrast, in recent years Britain would have been faced with deflationary pressures, which it again would not have been free to combat with monetary policy.

The fallacy in this argument about Britain being helpless on the seas of international finance is that there are two instruments of macroeconomic policy, not one. As well as monetary policy, there is fiscal policy. Everyone complained (at least in retrospect, even if some were silent at the time) about the failure of Chancellor Gordon Brown to maintain his early disciplined fiscal stance after Labour was re-elected in 2001. There were large and growing budget deficits leading to a turnround in the ratio of public debt/GDP, which began increasing again during the years of golden global growth.

Suppose that Britain had been in the Euro. Yes, it would have had easier monetary policy and lower interest rates. To prevent the lower interest rates being translated into excess demand, and thus inflation, the government would have been under pressure to raise taxes and/or cut down on the growth of public expenditure. Budget deficits would thus have been smaller (or non-existent), and the debt/GDP ratio would have grown less rapidly, or more likely continued to decline.[2]

Come 2008, when sterling depreciated to a rate weaker than the rate the British economy would have had in the Euro, the picture is less clear. Interest rates would still have been lower, so the easier monetary policy would have stimulated demand. On the other hand, foreign demand would have increased less. One cannot say a priori whether one would have needed a more expansionary fiscal policy to sustain demand or not.

What one can be certain of is that Britain would have been in a far stronger position to face the current crisis. It would have had less public debt and thus a lower debt/GDP ratio. And in most of the interim it would have had an unambiguously stronger balance of payments on current account, and would therefore have a stronger net wealth position vis-à-vis the rest of the world.

That is why the contention that Britain would have suffered from fixing its exchange rate at a sensible level vis-à-vis those neighbours with whom we do most of our trade strikes me as completely unfounded. It resulted in skewing our fiscal/monetary mix in a fundamentally undesirable way, in going on an irresponsible splurge of fiscal spending, and in indebting ourselves to the rest of the world. Britain is now paying the price.

John Williamson - Senior Fellow, Peterson Institute for International Economics.

---

2   If the fiscal tightening had exactly offset the lower interest rates resulting from being in the Euro, then growth (or at least demand-side growth) would have been unaffected. That is why growth is not discussed in this essay: it is irrelevant. (There are more subtle long-term supply-side effects, but practically everyone would agree that these argue in favour of British membership.)

Appendix to David Lea

Appendix to David Lea

The Rt Hon Gordon Brown MP, Chancellor of the Exchequer

Introduction

In thanking you for giving me the opportunity to address this conference on the Euro, let me first of all pay tribute to the trade union Movement for what is at the starting point of any discussion of Europe, and that is the internationalism of British trade unionism during a century or more of its existence.

Even from its modest beginnings in the late 19th Century, the trade union Movement was at the forefront of the British movement to end colonialism. British trade unionists led in the fight against fascism in Spain in the 1930s; and British trade unionists were at the head of the fight against apartheid from the 1950s onwards. I am pleased to say that today British trade unionists are very much part of the campaign which has been waged to deal with the problems of international debt and international poverty. Since the mid-1980s, it has been British working people and the trade unions who have been the principal leaders in putting the case for Europe.

It was the trade unions with local authorities who led the fight for British regional funds from the European Union. It has been the British trade union Movement which has led the fight for a social dimension in Europe and, of course, British trade unionists led the fight for the Social Chapter. As John said, I was pleased that one of the first acts of the Labour Government was to announce that we would sign the

Social Chapter on behalf of Britain.

More recently, it has been British trade unions and the British Labour Movement which have been seeking to make Europe a people's Europe. Of course, when it comes to Eastern Europe, it is the internationalism of the TUC and the trade unions in our country which has led us to help trade unionists in Eastern Europe to prepare for the new realities that the enlargement of the European Union will bring. This has all happened because of a central insight of trade unionism, the recognition of shared needs, mutual interest and linked destinies which bind working people together everywhere. It is because of that that we have had a wider vision of Britain in Europe, a Britain that is not isolated as some people would have it, but internationalist, a Britain that is not detached but a Britain which is engaged in Europe, a Britain not on the margins but a Britain right at the centre of Europe, a Britain that is co-operating, that is engaging and a Britain which is leading in Europe.

I believe that this conference today is very much part of this process. The trade union Movement is again leading the debate about the next stage of European development and what it means for working people in this country.

I am very pleased that you have with you as speakers today not just Euro MPs but speaking later will be Neil Kinnock, and I want to pay tribute to the work which Neil Kinnock has done not just as leader of the Labour Party during the ten years from 1983 but for the work which he has done as a European Commissioner. He has put the issues of transport, the integration of transport and the coordination of transport provision across Europe right at the heart of the European agenda.

It is because of Neil and you that we have in the past two years moved a long way from the debate which had been taking place in Britain before 1997. All of us can remember the debate about the Social Chapter and the Tory claims about job losses. Do you remember the

*Euro***Briefing**

'Unions and the Euro'
Special Issue - No. 8
July 1999

claim that 400,000 paper boys were going to lose their jobs as a result of the implementation of the Social Chapter? Do you remember the claim that the Social Chapter that had been signed by Helmut Kohl was a Marxist conspiracy which was being imposed on the United Kingdom? Remember all of the comments by Michael Howard when he was Employment Minister at the time. It is now saying something for the modern Conservative Party that you can imagine Michael Howard's resignation from the Front Bench of the Conservative Party to be a loss to the Tory Party in the House of Commons!

I remember taking part in a debate at that time with a Conservative MEP. The interviewer from the BBC kept saying all the time, "Why are you so negative about Europe? Why is everything in Europe forcing you to be so unconstructive and so negative?" Eventually, in frustration, the interviewer said to the Tory Euro MP, "What is it? Is it ignorance or apathy?", to which the guy said, "I don't know and I don't care".

People ask me what it is like after two years in government attending all of these European and international conferences. I have to tell you that it is partly reinforced by what happened yesterday in America with the resignation of Robert Rubin, who has been a brilliant Treasury Secretary during an American period of high growth and high employment.

I went to the first meeting of what was the G8 Group of Finance Ministers almost two weeks after I became Chancellor of the Exchequer. Before I arrived at the G8 meeting, one Finance Minister had already been sacked, so the original eight had become seven. I went to the next meeting a few weeks later and they were down to six. Then the Japanese Finance Minister went and it was down to five. Now in the G8, of the original eight Finance Ministers, there are only two left, and you will see why I do not want to be away from Downing Street for too long.

It reminded me of the advice I received the minute I came into the Treasury,

when a civil servant said to me, "You know, there are only two kinds of Finance Minister. There are those who fail and there are those who get out just in time". You can see why I am struggling to find the third way.

As we face the next challenge of Europe, to build an economic policy that ensures a dynamic, job creating economy and a fair society, I believe that in the building of that economic policy, Britain and British working people can lead again.

The challenge which John Monks set on Sunday in *The Observer* in an article he wrote is the European way in which social justice and economic progress can go hand in hand. Thechallenge, in fact, in looking at European economic policy, is to realise in the modern world of what is a global marketplace the central economic and social objectives that have underpinned our history for all these years since 1945, our commitment to high and stable levels of growth and employment.

The United States has job creation without, however, achieving the levels of social cohesion that they and others want. Europe has social cohesion but for many years, as we know, it has failed in job creation. Seventeen million men and women in Europe are today, tragically, unemployed.

I start from the view that to achieve these objectives, high and stable levels of growth and employment, enterprise and fairness, not only go together but they depend on each other in the modern world, and that our solution to these problems of unemployment depends on applying policies for both economic progress and social justice.

I believe that it is in this context, in building a strong economy and a fair society, to meet these objectives of the 1940s, that the debate about Europe's future should be taking place. It is in that context, too, that all the arguments about monetary union should be put forward and examined. Today, in addressing these questions, in my brief introduction to this conference, I want to answer those who wrongly, in my view, believe Britain does best when we

*Euro*Briefing

'Unions and the Euro'
Special Issue - No. 8
July 1999

unions and the euro The Rt Hon Gordon Brown MP, Chancellor of the Exchequer

stand alone, that Britain is far better free from long-term continental attachments, and I want to answer those who claim that joining Europe is some sort of wrong turning point and those who believe that our traditional way of life and our sovereignty are submerged and, therefore, our future lies outside of Europe.

I want to argue instead that in engaging constructively with Europe, as trade unionists have done over these recent years, is our best way forward, that British values have much to contribute to the development of this new Europe and that the new European way, to be successful and to mark out Europe in the world, must combine our commitments to economic progress with our dedication to social cohesion and social justice.

So we start from these objectives of the 1940s - high and stable levels of growth and employment, which are as pressing in the new conditions of the modern world as they were in the years after 1944. I believe that to achieve these objectives, in a modern and global marketplace, which is quite distinct from the circumstances of the 1940s, we now need to do two things together. First of all, we must build a solid foundation of economic stability and, secondly, we must develop a policy with job creation which will require economic reform.

*Euro***Briefing**

'Unions and the Euro'
Special Issue - No. 8
July 1999

Stability

First, how do we achieve that stability and the importance of the debate about monetary union to that? Let us remember how much the world has changed. The post-1945 world was a world of closed financial markets. There were few financial flows between countries. Today, we live in a quite different economy - rapid international financial flows running into billions of dollars every day. The lesson is that investment will only come to those countries which show that they can pursue policies which achieve economic stability. It is because of that fact that so much emphasis has to be placed on achieving monetary and fiscal stability.

Today growth and employment cannot come through the rigid application of monetary targets within one country and, in my view, it never could. Nor, however, can growth and employment be guaranteed by the old methods of fine tuning behind national borders irrespective of what is happening in the rest of the world, that fine tuning which, in its later days, failed to recognise that there is no longer a trade off between inflation and growth. Instead, in my view, growth and employment and a stability on which they are founded will come, first of all, from setting out clear long-term policy objectives; secondly, from clearly and well-understood, predictable, rules for monetary and fiscal policies and, thirdly, from an openness which keeps markets properly informed and ensures that institutions and objectives are credible.

It is because of that that in Britain's case, when we came to power in 1997, we created a new monetary policy for what are new times and new challenges. It was for these long-term reasons that we made the Bank of England independent whilst we set the inflation target. It was because of that that we set the rules under which the Bank of England would work, how interest rate decisions were to be made, the voting system, the reporting system and the communicating system, and it is because of that, also - the we need to achieve stability so that we can have the investment funds needed for jobs and growth - that we also set out a new fiscal policy for the public finances. The golden rule that current expenditures were paid for by current revenues over the cycle, the sustainable investment rule that you should borrow for much needed investment in your economy, clear procedures, the three year - not the one year commitment - long term commitment to spending settlements, and again an openness in the debate about public services and public spending, a proper system of disclosure in what we have called the Code of Fiscal Stability.

That is what we did in Britain to meet the challenges of the new world.

In mainland Europe the same search for

this macro economic stability, which is absolutely critical if any country is going to succeed in the modern world, is to be pursued through monetary union. The same pressures are having to be responded to, the pressures of the global marketplace, the same lessons are having to be learned, that you cannot return to the failed methods of the 1980s and, of course in Europe, to achieve that stability upon which growth and employment depend, they have developed a policy of monetary stability through the creation of an independent European Central Bank and a single currency, the Stability and Growth Pact of the European Union to achieve fiscal sustainability and, side by side, of course, we have the discussions in the debate now taking place about a more dynamic job creating economy for Europe. This is the European road to stability.

Through a single currency, intended as it does to remove unnecessary currency speculation within Europe, to reduce transaction costs which are a barrier and a big expense to business often at the expense of employment and, of course, the aim is to keep long-term interest rates low. These are the objectives which are being pursued to achieve that goal of 1944 that we have stable levels of growth and employment. So the single currency is born out of this changed economic environment, it is built on the platform of stability, up and working in Europe over the last five months, it is, indeed, clearly reducing currency transaction costs, within Europe it is curbing currency speculation, which has done so much damage in the past and it has led to interest rates coming down.

We are the first British government to declare for the principle of that monetary union.

We are the first to state that there is no overriding constitutional barrier to membership. We are the first to make clear and unambiguous economic benefit to Britain the decisive test as to whether we should join or not, and we are the first to engage in helping make a single currency in Europe work, to offer constructive and practical support

to our European partners so that we can create more employment and more prosperity. Of course, the single currency raises important constitutional questions. It raises questions about the sharing of economic sovereignty. These are questions which this Government will not and should not run away from.

But those who say that there is an insuperable constitutional objection to a single currency have, in my view, failed to take on board the fact that where a pooling of political and economic sovereignty has been in the British interests, as in the United Nations, NATO and in the existing Single Market of the European Union, we have been willing, in the national interest, to embrace it in the past. This Government, having declared for the principle of monetary union, the real question which we are now addressing, since the statement we made to the House of Commons in 1997, is whether the single currency is in practical terms in our national economic interest; in other words, whether there are clear and unambiguous economic benefits. So we have committed ourselves to make economic advantage the decisive test.

We have set out five clear economic tests which affect the jobs, prosperity and the industries of this country, and these tests are the following.

First, whether there can, to make a single currency work, be sustainable convergence between Britain and the economies of the single currency. So the practical test, the test which has to be met, is that we need to be confident that the United Kingdom's economic cycle, which has been subject in the past to boom and bust, has converged with that of other European countries and whether this convergence is likely to be sustained for the British economy to have the stability which is needed and the prosperity which would come from a common European monetary policy.

The second test is also a clear and obvious one and it is practical; whether there is sufficient flexibility to cope with all the economic change? So the practical test is that to be successful in a

*Euro***Briefing**

'Unions and the Euro'
Special Issue · No. 8
July 1999

unions and the euro The Rt Hon Gordon Brown MP, Chancellor of the Exchequer

monetary union, Britain would need to be able to adjust to change and adjust to unexpected economic events in any part of that monetary union. To deal with some of the challenges we face in Britain, the Government have begun to implement a programme for investing in education, helping people move from unemployment into work and improving the workings of the capital markets for new investment in our country.

That leads me on to the third test. It must be good for investment. So the practical test is that we need to be confident that joining EMU will bring better conditions for industry to make the long term decisions we want them to make, to raise what has been over a long period of time an unacceptably low rate of investment in the British economy. That test involves confidence in what is going to happen to interest rates in the monetary union, that they should be low to encourage the investment that is needed and confidence also that we have investment mechanisms for getting the investment to the industries which need them.

The fourth test is the effect on a growing sector of the economy in terms of jobs as well as in terms of wealth, and that is the financial services industry which exists in Britain. Clearly, monetary union will affect that industry more directly and more immediately than any other sectors of the economy, and we are confident that the United Kingdom has the potential to see that industry thrive in or out of monetary union so long as we are properly prepared. However, the practical test is whether the benefits of new opportunities from a single currency could be easier to tap for the jobs in our financial services industries from within the eurozone. We can therefore strengthen our position and the jobs which come from it as a leading financial centre in Europe.

The fifth test which we have set is a test that everyone here would want to be right at the centre of any decision, and indeed which brings all of the other parts of the decision together, and that

is whether it is good for employment. For this Government, and I believe for the trade union Movement, this is the most practical test, and how employment creating measures in other areas must be accompanied clearly by benefits from the single currency itself. Ultimately, the test must be whether that single currency is good for jobs. These are the tests which we will examine during the coming years.

Preparations

As you can see, economic and monetary union presents British industry and British people with many challenges. Our view has been that, instead of the old wait and see attitude which came from the last government, we must make the preparations which are necessary to allow us to make a genuine decision, subject to a referendum of the people of this country. So our policy is, therefore, not wait and see but it is to prepare and then decide.

Last year when we commissioned a survey, we found that only 30 per cent offirms thought they needed to prepare for the Euro and only five per cent had done anything. As a result of a series of recommendations, we decided to tackle this matter directly through a national advertising campaign and direct mailing of companies. Twice as many businesses are now making preparations, there are 12 Euro forums in every region of the country. We have put in place arrangements to enable firms to pay taxes, file accounts and issue and re-dominate shares, receive certain agricultural grants and grants under Regional Selective Assistance in euros.

In February, as many of you know, we published an outline national changeover plan which set out all the practical steps which would be needed for the UK to join the euro. We set out the stage by stage procedures setting out the practical implications of changing to the euro and giving advice to companies and workforces on the way to take forward preparations. I am conscious that if we are to make these preparations, the public sector must take a lead and every government

*Euro*Briefing

'Unions and the Euro'
Special Issue - No. 8
July 1999

The Rt Hon Gordon Brown MP, Chancellor of the Exchequer **unions and the euro**

department is now playing its part. We have long thought it absolutely crucial and critical that the trade union Movement is directly involved in the preparations process.

John Monks is on the Standing Committee on euro preparations. David Lea is on the Business Advisory Group, and I am grateful for their contributions. I hope that the trade unions will continue to be actively involved right at the heart of ensuring that British industry and British workforces are prepared.

Economic reform

Ensuring a foundation of economic stability is central to meeting our economic objectives of high and stable levels of growth and employment. It is a necessary condition of success. You have to look at new ways of doing that in the conditions we find in the 1990s, but of course it is not a sufficient condition of a successful economy. In a successful economic policy, we need to get both macro economic policy and supply side policy right. It is not enough for economic policy to fly on one wing. We need it to fly on both wings. Hence, our stress not only on stability but on the certain element of a European economic policy, and that is job creation which has to be accompanied by economic reform.

Europe has 17 millions unemployed. Five million young people are out of work. Five million men and women are long-term unemployed. Whilst 10 per cent of the unemployed in the United States have been unemployed for more than a year, nearly 50 per cent of Europe's unemployed are long-term unemployed. So we have a major challenge ahead if we are to create a dynamic job creating economy and if we are to solve this problem of long-term structural unemployment.

We know enough now to recognise that in a fast-changing world of constant innovation, the real issue is how government can equip people for the challenges of the future. The role of government is not to stop the clock or

to freeze the brain and say that everything can continue all the time as it was, nor is the role of government, as happened under the previous administration, to leave people defenceless against the huge global forces of change. The role of government is to help equip people to master these changes. That is the basis of our New Deal strategy in Britain which is now being discussed in Europe. It is designed to help those very groups that right across Europe have lost out as a result of technological and employment change - the young, lone parents, the long-term unemployed, the disabled - to offer them opportunities for the training and skills necessary to work. There are signs that in Britain this strategy is already starting to work. I can say today that youth unemployment is 56 per cent down on its level at the General Election and long-term unemployment has now fallen by 42 per cent since May 1997.

Central to job creation is a commitment to equip people for change by investing in education and training, and recognising that 80 per cent of those who will be in the labour force 10 years from now are already in the workforce today. Even in the most business conscious countries in Europe, only a fraction of today's workforce are upgrading their skills. Across Europe we have to do far more in lifelong learning, and in Britain we believe that the start we have made with the proposed University for Industry, Individual Learning Accounts for a million workers are the best ways forward to give people the lifelong educational skills which they need.

Creating new opportunities for work and then for education, training and skills must also be complemented by another measure, and that is to make work pay. To move people from poverty out of work to poverty in work is simply unacceptable. That is why we have begun to address the problem with radical reforms of the tax and benefits system, building on the minimum wage, building for families on Child Benefit and with a new tax and benefits structure which means that some low

*Euro*Brief**ing**

'Unions and the Euro'
Special Issue - No. 8
July 1999

unions and the euro The Rt Hon Gordon Brown MP, Chancellor of the Exchequer

paid families in this country in October will be receiving £40 to £50 a week more.

So the way forward is not simply to cling to the old systems which cannot cope with a world of technological change, or to leave people ill-equipped and powerless in the face of these insecurities, but it is an active welfare state, new tax and benefit system, a modern employment policy centred on new opportunities for work, and I believe that in Europe we are now starting to make progress.

As a central element of our British Presidency, we pushed forward work on European employment plans, and we called for national action plans, initiated by us, agreed at the Luxembourg Summit. Every country now draws them up. The first set of European employment guidelines have now been published, the national employment action plans show what each Member State is doing in concrete terms and how they are sharing best practice to achieve it. Each individual country now has to set down how they will get young unemployed men and women back into the labour force and showing how, after six months, they all get opportunities, how they will get the long-term unemployed back into work and how, after a year, a person who has been unemployed will get new opportunities and into work. The next set of action plans which will take this further will be submitted by our Member States early next year.

This is just the beginning of the new approach to employment. A top priority willbe to consider the lessons from the employment action plans so that we can have a real debate on the best means of getting unemployment down in Europe. No one country can never have all the answers to all the problems of tackling unemployment and raising employment. We want to learn from each other as to how we can make progress.

We welcome the initiative for an Employment Pact of European Union countries to further our commitments to create the conditions for high and stable levels of employment and growth. My European colleagues agree with me about the importance of economic reform in Europe for job creation and that is why the title of the Pact to reflect the role of economic reform will be "The European Employment Pact - Closer Cooperation to Boost Employment and Economic Reforms in Europe".

That set of employment measures needs to be backed up by a strong regional policy and a strong social policy in Europe too. That is why we took action to deliver the Social Chapter for Britain, that is why in March at the Berlin European Council we fought for the European Structural Funds for the regions of the United Kingdom to back up our employment policies, and that is why West Wales and the Valleys, South Yorkshire and Cornwall, as well as Merseyside, will now receive Objective 1 funding. It is why Northern Ireland now has a unique package of support and why we secured funding equivalent to Objective 1 status for the Highlands and Islands. After negotiations in Berlin, more than double the number of people in Britain will be covered by regional structural funds compared with only 6.5 million under the original European Commission proposals.

Of course Europe needs to modernise as we are modernising. We want Europe to be more open, more competitive, more adaptable and flexible to set its sights on moving beyond the sterile debate between regulation and deregulation with a new emphasis on skills, productivity and employment opportunity. Europe needs structural economic reforms alongside the other measures I have mentioned.

One area is competition policy, because in Europe there is too much monopoly at the expense of ordinary working people. We must reform the product markets in Europe to help Europe become more dynamic and competitive and we must also reform our capital markets to enable investment funds to get to the job creating projects which need them. We need policies which offer greater competition in the product markets through an extension of

*Euro**Briefing***

'Unions and the Euro'
Special Issue - No. 8
July 1999

competition to attack cartels, monopolies and vested interests which still dominate too much of the marketplace in Europe and prevent the creation of jobs.

In terms of creating new investment policies in Europe, in addition to the European Investment Bank and the other funds which have been created around it, we want to see progress on the venture capital industry in Europe, the challenge to create a strong venture capital industry so that high technology firms which get support in financing and create jobs in America get exactly the same kind of support in Europe.

Despite having the biggest single market in the world, European businesses are still too dependent on bank loans and overdrafts and have problems in obtaining the investment funds they need. So in Europe we need a new approach to investment to increase the number of businesses, to raise the survival rate of small and medium sized businesses, to destroy all the barriers which exist - fiscal, regulatory, economic and cultural, as a matter of urgency to job creation.

In this way, we can build a new Europe with a tradition of social partnership, a Europe that is better equipped to meet the needs of a modern global economy, which can create the investment and then the employment which is necessary to get the best for people and to get the people to be in a position to realise their potential to the full.

Context

Let me, finally, put our European policy in its proper context. To those who believe that Britain does best when isolated and detached, let me say that my experience is that the opposite is true. While Britain's relationship with Europe has neither been exclusive nor constant, any study of our history shows not just that we have always been a European power but that Britain has been European for good pragmatic reasons. Britain did not and would not at any point this century relinquish our role in Europe or abdicate our

responsibility for the progress of the continent. Europe, by virtue of geography and history, is where we are. Fifty per cent of our trade is with Europe. Our approach must always, in my view, be guided by a common sense engagement in pursuit of the national interest with all the impact it has for jobs and prosperity in our country.

The idea that we could now, in 1999, withdraw from Europe or go outside of Europe's mainstream and become a sort of Hong Kong of Europe, a low wage competitor with the Far East, or some sort of Tory dream which is a tax haven servicing major trading blocks, the idea that Britain was some sort of Greater Guernsey, only needs a minute's consideration to be rejected. Britain, which has been a first rank European power for centuries, often holding the balance of power in Europe, would become under these suggestions a spectator in Europe's future development.

It is through a close constructive relationship with our European partners that Britain will not only enjoy greater prosperity but continue to have influence and continue to make a contribution on the world stage. The more influence we have through Europe in Paris and Bonn, the more influence we will have in Washington and elsewhere.

To those who say that the Atlantic Alliance is in contradiction with our European commitments, I say, again, that the opposite is true. Britain's interests in the rest of the world are best served by being strong in Europe.

History suggests to me that there are no grounds for believing that to be pro-British it is necessary to be anti-European. Indeed, history suggests to me that far from being isolationist, Britain always thrives when it is outward looking and internationalist.

I believe that British values have a great deal to offer Europe as it develops. Being in and leading in Europe means that we can contribute British ideas to the development of the European Union and the British qualities which will help Europe to develop in the

*Euro*Briefing

'Unions and the Euro'
Special Issue - No. 8
July 1999

9

future are our openness and our willingness to look outwards, our internationalist instincts, the connections we have which stretch right across the world, our creativity and adaptability as a nation, our insistence on the importance of public service and openness in the running of institutions, and the other values we share with other countries, namely, the importance of valuing work, fairness and opportunity for all.

These are qualities which we can bring to British engagement with Europe. These are the qualities which can help the nations of Europe go forward together into a more prosperous 21st Century. So, to those who say that the future means Britain being submerged in Europe, I say, again, that quite the opposite is true. With an emphasis on these British qualities, Europe can learn from Britain just as we in Britain can learn from the rest of Europe.

So the British way forward, the way in which trade unionists in this country have always chosen, is not to retreat into some narrow insularity, some defensive isolationism, but it is to be open, confidently outward looking, to lead by example. This internationalism has always been at the heart of both the principles and the practices of trade unionism in Britain. As we prepare for the future, this internationalism is what we must practise in Europe now. Thank you.

*Euro***Briefing**

'Unions and the Euro'
Special Issue - No. 8
July 1999